SHAKESPEARE'S EARLY HISTORY PLAYS

Also by Donald G. Watson and also published by Macmillan

READING PHILIP ROTH (editor with Asher Z. Milbauer)

Shakespeare's Early History Plays

Politics at Play on the Elizabethan Stage

DONALD G. WATSON

Professor of English
Florida International University, Miami

MACMILLAN
LONDON

First published 1990

Published by
THE MACMILLAN PRESS LTD
Houndmills, Basingstoke, Hampshire RG21 2XS
and London

Companies and representatives
throughout the world

**Printed in Great Britain by
Billing & Sons Ltd, Worcester**

British Library Cataloguing in Publication Data
Watson, Donald, G.
Shakespeare's early history plays: politics at play
on the Elizabethan stage.
1. Drama in English. Shakespeare, William. Historical
plays – Critical studies
I. Title
822.3'3
ISBN 0–333–49881–X

for Abigail and Nancy

Contents

Acknowledgements

Quotations from Shakespeare's early history plays are from the Arden editions – *King Henry VI, Parts 1, 2 & 3*, edited by Andrew S. Cairncross, *King Henry III*, edited by Antony Hammond, and *King John*, edited by E. A. J. Honigman – with the permission of Methuen and Company Ltd.

Quotations from all other Shakespeare plays are from *The Riverside Shakespeare*, edited by G. Blakemore Evans, and are used with the permission of Houghton Mifflin Company.

Preface

When Henry James wanted to create a great stride forward in the theatrical abilities of Miriam Rooth, the ambitious actress and heroine of *The Tragic Muse*, he gave her the role of Constance from Shakespeare's *King John* to rehearse and to master. With relish and with talent, Miriam takes to the fury, wrath, and irony of the part, amazing the sophisticated connoisseur of the theater, Peter Sherringham, with her emotional range and histrionic subtleties. Miriam sees Constance just a notch below Juliet and Cleopatra as the most desirable characters she might impersonate on the stage, and James clearly admired the "poetry" of Constance's passionate lamentations:

> The powerful, ample manner in which Miriam handled her scene produced its full impression, the art with which she surmounted its difficulties, the liberality with which she met its great demand upon the voice, and the variety of expression that she threw into a torrent of objurgation. It was a real composition, studded with passages that called a suppressed "Brava!" to the lips and seeming to show that a talent capable of such an exhibition was capable of any thing.

James's novel reminds us that other ages regarded *King John* with much more admiration than we do. That reminder in itself will come as no great revelation, peppered as is the history of Shakespearean production and criticism with surprising evaluations and interpretations; still it calls us to be more skeptical of our own judgments. James's Miriam also points to the highly theatrical manner of early Shakespeare: again, not a revelation but a useful reminder that in reading the early history plays in the study or classroom we may forget their origins in the theater, their existence *as* plays. If the taste for melodrama was greater in 1890 than now, Constance realizes her "power" as a character only on stage when played by a young and talented actress.

James's conception of Miriam Rooth reminds us finally of the nature of drama as a representation of life through the playing out of a collection of roles and a script by actors in an auditorium, but a representation which also suggests that life itself *is* acting: "All the world's a stage." The theatrical stage always erases the boundaries of life and art by suggesting the improvisational qualities of both: life as self-presentation, as choosing among roles to play. Sherringham discovers that Miriam makes no distinctions:

> It came over him suddenly that so far from there being any question of her having the histrionic nature, she simply had it in such perfection that she was always acting; that her existence was a series of parts assumed for the moment, each changed for the next, before the perpetual mirror of some curiosity or admiration or wonder – some spectatorship that she perceived or imagined to the people about her . . . . It struck him abruptly that a woman whose only being was to "make believe," to make believe that she had any and every being that you liked, that would serve a purpose, produce a certain effect, and whose identity resided in the continuity of her personations, so that she had no moral privacy, as he phrased it to himself, but lived in a high wind of exhibition, of figuration – such a woman was a kind of monster, in whom of necessity there would be nothing to like, because there would be nothing to take hold of.

Although Miriam's "series of personations" presents an extreme form of life as theatrical performance, it illustrates the monstrous opposition of the theater to the permanence of role, character, and identity assumed by traditional social norms and moral expectations.

In Shakespeare's age one of the opposites of the improvisational is the institutional and iconic – the staged display of fixed meanings and roles. These displays also partake of the nature of the theatrical but not the dramatic; they are meant to represent qualities and values actually present in the role played out by the actor who *is* the role; unlike the theatrical stage, the political and social stage does not distinguish between identity and performance and thereby limits the audience's interpretation to a passive acceptance of the signs and symbols displayed. The day before her coronation Elizabeth I arranged the meanings of her passage from London to Westminster; an anonymous spectator wrote that "if a man shoulde say well, he could not better tearme the Citie of London that time, than as a stage wherein was shewed the wonderful spectacle, of a noble hearted Princesse toward her most loving People . . . . "

Throughout her reign Elizabeth fashioned numerous spectacles of this kind, but these were intended to reveal her nature as "prince-like" rather than her impersonation of the Prince. The essays which follow attempt to explore both the connections between the theatricality of the stage and the theatrical staging of Elizabethan power and the always potentially subversive expression of a dramatic, historical, and improvisational, view of reality in Shakespeare's early history plays within a highly theatrical, iconic, and ideological culture. Between the representational art of the stage and the visual presentation of authority, hierarchy, and power lie the complexities of actual practices and beliefs whose own modes of representation are often obscure and hidden but which clearly emerge in those moments in which the series of personations demand our attention equally with the iconic displays and reveal in moments of confrontation and irony the dynamic and ambivalent nature of political action. From these moments Shakespeare makes plays of politics by disclosing the politics at play in English history, both past and contemporary.

1

Theatre, History, Politics

THEATRICAL DIMENSIONS OF THE DRAMATIC TEXT

Shakespeare's history plays have been attracting more and more of their fair share of scholarly attention in recent years, but less often than comedies and tragedies are the histories discussed critically from a theatrical perspective. Enlightening studies of their dramaturgical strengths and weaknesses do, of course, exist, but consideration of their technical achievement is far outweighed by examinations of their topical politics, theological issues, world pictures, and ideas of kingship – all most carefully placed against the historical background of Elizabethan England in the 1590s. We can know them as embodiments of Renaissance ideas of political morality, as mirrors of Elizabethan policy, as essays upon the relationship of family and state, as meditations upon the king's two bodies, as rituals of the ethic of order, as warnings against rebellion, as dramatic treatises about the Tudor myth, as inquiries into the concept of divine providence, as formal developments of the chronicle and morality play, as explorations of the historian's art. We can know their sources and analyze the playwright's manipulation of events and personages, memorize genealogical charts, and map out the battles. And we can do much more to know the history plays *as* plays.

The following pages are based upon the assumption that Shakespeare's plays demand a critical approach which does not merely adapt the methods through which we come to understand the lyric and the narrative.[1] At least in our academic classrooms, drama in general has suffered from our concentration upon the poetic textures of its language and the psychologies of motivation and behavior. Though images and characters form essential components of dramatic literature, we too readily seize upon the most accessible literary aspects of great plays and yield to the leisurely experience of the study when the excitement of the

1

theater is unavailable. Established by expert editors, the texts of
the Shakespearean canon provide a security which critics from Dr.
Johnson to Lamb to Wilson Knight have preferred to the impurities
and disappointments of actual performance.

My discussions of Shakespeare's early English history plays
attempt to foster an awareness of and attention to their theatrical
dimensions as an essential element of understanding them fully
and as a fundamentally inseparable part of their meaning and
artistry, though a part certainly interdependent upon the linguistic
and narrative aspects fixed upon the page. The texts themselves
always remain my single point of reference, the visual and auditory
implications of which my comments are meant to "discover" in the
Elizabethan sense.

The history plays belong to the theater, and academic scholarship offering interpretations which cannot be directed and acted
should be regarded with even more suspicion than actual productions which become indefensible when compared with what
Shakespeare wrote. To have some idea of what an individual
scene looks and sounds like is crucial to our understanding of
its meaning and artistry, more essential than is Holinshed or
the homilies of 1547 and 1571. Because most of us do not get
to see even the popular histories performed very often, we must
work at a theatrical understanding; we readers must perform
their texts by imagining them in performance. But we can educate our theatrical imaginations by reading records of stage history and by learning more about the stage and the society of
Shakespeare's time. Our own theatrical experiences, of course,
provide another source to call upon, and the texts themselves
bristle with explicit and implicit information about staging and
acting.

One can never come near being definitive about the visual and
aural, temporal and spatial, dimensions of drama, but not to
risk appearing to be hopelessly subjective about the extra-verbal
dimensions of Shakespeare's art is to forego much of the artistic
complexity of his theater. The rest of this introduction examines
some of the difficulties and advantages of making this attempt to
integrate a theatrical and especially an audience-centered criticism
with a more traditional interpretive approach. Every performance
– whether in the theater, the classroom, or the reader's mind –
is simply another interpretation; it is not the text, but like every
interpretation, it offers us at least the possibility of illuminating

some part of the text, even if only by sending us there again to prove its wrongheadedness.

All of these approaches to a theatrical criticism of Shakespeare's plays can tell us something of his dramaturgical skills, but each has its limitations. One's approach must recognize these and must be as eclectic as possible if it is to capture the dynamic nature of the energy of performance inherent in the text. At the least, an awareness of the theatrical dimensions of the plays will constrain our interpretive imaginations, inhibiting analysis and evaluation based upon untheatrical criteria. Yet, even so we must take care. Our own memories, and the opinions of journalistic and academic reviewers, are highly selective. We have only to reflect for a moment to realize that even our own direct experiences of Shakespeare in performance very often provide us with the most general impressions and the most specific details: we remember a production with approval or disapprobation and its specific moments or particular choices as good or bad ideas. For example, I admired Maggie Smith's Cleopatra at the 1976 Stratford, Ontario, festival: witty, charming, sensual, she surprised me since I doubted that the thin, redheaded Miss Jean Brodie could play a convincing Cleopatra. However, I find it virtually impossible now to recall exactly how her readings of specific scenes varied from my expectations, though I am sure they did. I do remember, alas, that Octavius's Roman soldiers wore white, belted tunics which resembled the pleated short skirts of the women tennis players I had seen earlier that day on the courts near the Avon and white, knee-length boots which seemed more appropriate for majorettes, go-go dancers, or streetwalkers. Why such inessential elements stick in our minds may be left to others, but one can note similar observations in even the most sophisticated reviews of productions.

Such vagaries of response teach us to mistrust the reports of others as well as ourselves and remind us that performances are the creatures of circumstance, conditioned by our own preconceptions, by the other *Anthony and Cleopatra*s we have seen, by the other appearances of actors and actresses, by the choices of director, designer, costumer, composer. I recall the perfect appropriateness of the bittersweet, Felliniesque music which added considerably to the melancholic festiveness of the 1978 Old Vic *Twelfth Night* and the excellence of the performances of Robert Eddison as Feste and Eileen Atkins as Viola. Though I liked the production very much for its consistency of tone and innovative staging of crucial scenes, it made me realize that one does not actually experience the director – in this case, Tony Richardson – except in retrospect or in radical adaptations, such as Peter Brook's 1970 *Midsummer Night's Dream* or John Barton's 1974 *King John*. However trivial, such insights offer valuable correctives to our current insistence upon the primacy of the director: if he is behind, he is rarely a part of our direct experience of the performance. With so much emphasis upon "the director's theater" in recent years, perhaps we need to be reminded that theatrical *regisseurs*, unlike film directors, do not control and construct the scale, distance, and point of view of seeing live actors. None can be *auteurs*, though some would wish to be.[2]

Shakespeare live remains ephemeral, the two or three hours' traffic of an evening, yet it can restore a sense of proportion difficult to obtain in the study. The "literary" critic may miss the stature and importance of the role of Warwick in *3 Henry VI* or of Buckingham in *Richard III* or of Northumberland in *Richard II* unless he has seen those plays acted. On the other hand, what had seemed so essential in the study can become tertiary or even startle us by its absence in the theater. Scholarship raises our consciousness of the long view advanced by Edward Hall and other historians, but the history plays in performance often betray our expectations about the Tudor myth. In the 1977 *3 Henry VI* at Stratford it was only fitfully present and then at the obvious moments, as in Henry's prophetic blessing of young Richmond.[3] *Richard III* in performance provides the audience with its presence: the Tudor myth is fully embodied in Queen Margaret but in a most perverted variation. When not completely omitted, Margaret embodies a striking distortion of the providential view of history, a constant parody of the Tudor myth. For this bitter, warped old Frenchwoman, providence means the deaths of all the enemies of the Lancasters. Is there a God who will not respond to her cries of vengeance? We should hope so. That her curses are actually fulfilled depends upon the effectiveness of human evil not upon providence. The violence and cruelty of her schematic retribution enforce our ambivalence about the providential view of history. In performance, her shrillness and singlemindedness may help redirect our critical emphases.

In the study one forgets such presences. We do not see or hear the silent presence of the king in the *Henry VI* plays, of Arthur in *King John*, of Bolingbroke in *Richard II*, nor of the others present in the

Tavern scenes in *1 Henry IV*, for whose benefit the impersonations, jokes, and flytings are staged by Hal and Falstaff as well as for the audience's. Seldom do Shakespeare's interpreters discuss the second part of III.1. in *1 Henry IV*, yet this leisurely conversation among Glendower, Hotspur, Mortimer, and the Ladies Percy and Mortimer stops the frenzied rush toward rebellion of the determined coalition of offended lords. As we see the pace of dramatic action slow, we hear Lady Mortimer speak and sing in Welsh, though the printed text provides her no actual words. "Peace, she sings," says Hotspur, and an absolute stillpoint of grace, beauty, and charm is created, a lyrical island in a stormy sea of political maneuvrings.[4] (I first heard this nontextual moment many years ago on the Marlowe Society recording with total surprise.) If we cannot listen to her song, we shall not only miss the artistry of the scene but also misinterpret the sequence it begins. Henry IV's confrontation with Hal follows, full of long detailed reproofs and "extenuations," and Falstaff's concern over debts and picked pockets follows that. The rebels have not been forgotten nor are these scenes without clear thematic parallels, but the rhythm of the political drama is not reestablished after the Welsh pause until Worcester, Douglas, and Hotspur open Act IV with what Falstaff refers to as the "brave world" of "rare words." The sequence deliberately postpones the inevitable battles, providing us with various indirect perspectives from which to understand the political plot.

Such observations and analyses – however incidental and fragmentary – should suggest the necessity of a theater-centered and especially an audience-centered criticism of Shakespeare's histories, of its value and its excitement in extending our understanding of these plays as plays. At least, these comments will serve to remind us of the literal facts of the theatrical experience: actors representing characters on a stage before a group of people who respond to their physical appearance, words, movements. The nature of this situation dictates not merely an obvious and possible model for dramatic interpretation but an essential one.

Our personal experiences of Shakespeare performed educate our imaginations to discover the theatrical dimensions of the printed texts, and to this radically limited theatergoing we may add research into an extensive variety of theater records of past productions. Such records are often scattered among many places and are of many kinds: the journalistic impressions in newspapers and monthlies, the director's pronouncements in playbills, an occasional interview by an actor, the unauthoritative promptbook, the private letters of famous members of an audience, the more extensive reviews of the *Shakespeare Survey* and *Shakespeare Quarterly*, the stage histories of modern scholars. Using this material is fraught with problems, the most obvious of which is its subjectivity. If we recognize our own memories as unreliable and highly selective, we must naturally suspect others' accounts: one seasoned critic's judgment sometimes even cancels out another's as each reveals as much of his own taste as details of performance. For example, both Roger Warren and David Daniell in lengthy reviews of the 1977 *Henry VI* plays point to the molehill scene – the murder of York by Margaret and Clifford in 3 *Henry VI* (I.4); Warren found it "curiously *un*moving," Daniell "as disturbing a thing as one can see."[5] But the interpreter of the theatrical dimensions of Shakespeare's plays does not seek to evaluate and rank productions but to extend his awareness of the possibilities of performances as interpretations of the multitude of potential realizations of the printed text in the theater. Were total reconstructions of the acting of Garrick or Kean or Benson feasible, they would tell us more about the actors and their times than about Shakespeare.

Production-centered criticism of Shakespeare generates theater history rather than theatrical criticism. An awareness of performance values, changing styles in the theater, directors' intentions, all these and much else sharpen our understanding of the implications of the text; if nothing else, even the shortest of journalistic reviews recreates the necessary model of someone responding to live actors on a stage. The analyses of performances, writes J. L. Styan, "have at least this claim to validity, that those devices of Elizabethan origin which can be made to work, those rhythms of speech, the flexing of character, illusion and the structural orchestration of the play, when tried upon a live audience assembled in conditions of theatre, are less open to the irrelevancies of impressionistic criticism for which the writer need consult no one other than himself."[6] For the Shakespearean scholar, too often have the details of performance recorded in theater records or reported by reviewers and stage historians appeared irrelevant to the author's text or the Elizabethanness of the original performance. Any number of these – compatible or incompatible with the printed speeches – could be compiled: the extensive use of extras in the nineteenth-century pageantry of the histories, the various methods of providing for Falstaff's bulk, the casting of young girls in the parts of Arthur and Prince Henry in *King John*. The traditions of casting and stage business similarly reveal very little beyond the conservatism of the theater; Hotspur's stammering, Richard II's blondness against Bolingbroke's darkness, Charles VI's senility in *Henry V*, and many other elements of characterization have no warrant in the text. The scholar will find equally unhelpful accounts of productions which confuse Shakespeare's ambivalent vision with current cynicism. In 1978 productions of *Richard III* in Washington, D.C., and Melbourne both suggested that Richmond differs very little, if at all, from Richard III; "we are never saved," wrote Jeanne Addison Roberts of the Folger Shakespeare Library's production, "we simply replace one variety of evil with another."[7] Likewise, cynicism replaced celebration in the 1971 RSC production of *Henry VIII*, director Trevor Nunn preferring the symmetry of the closed circle to the "wonders" Cranmer "speakest"; in his review, J. W. Lambert says:

> As he [Henry VIII] opened the play with the defiant gaze from the darkness, so after the splendour of the christening . . . blazing with gold and silver, bright with bells, as the court withdrew, so the darkness closed in upon him again and left him still staring out – at the future, and this time with a look something very like horror upon his face.[8]

Granted the ephemeral and imperfect nature of Shakespearean production, its dependence upon commercial interests and financial resources, directors' eccentricities, actors' idiosyncrasies, the composition of repertory companies, the pressure to make it new and contemporary, and the winds of history, consciously or unconsciously felt, what can we learn from reading the notoriously subjective accounts of reviewers and pouring through the miscellaneous records of theater history? The trivia of inflatable rubber suits, the incomprehensibility of girls in boys' roles, and the violations of the obvious intentions of the printed text remain in our minds, but can we ignore the experience of those who actually *do* rather than merely *read* Shakespeare? One particular example comes to mind, especially since it highlights a controversial scene from a seldomly acted history play. In *3 Henry VI* Shakespeare includes a scene (II.5) in which a "Son that hath kill'd his father" enters at one door with the body and a "Father that hath kill'd his son, at another door, bearing of his son" (S.D., 54,78). The historical critic will find such business a throw-back to the Morality play tradition;

the structural critic may find it unnecessary to the plot, themes, and characterizations; the stylistic critic may find its formality out of keeping with the rest of the play. No doubt, the scene's theatricality is primitive, but how does an audience react to it? In producing the Henry VI plays in 1952 at the Birmingham Repertory Theatre, Sir Barry Jackson considered cutting the entire scene, but then decided to stage it. The scene proved, he writes, very effective, illustrating the dramatist's method once more "infallible." It offered a "still tableau" which fixed the disorder and sadness of civil war visually for the spectators, who, he reports, found it quite moving.[9] If we take such accounts seriously at all, we will return to our text and re-examine it. The scene opens with Henry VI's soliloquizing about his woes and those he has brought to England. The theatrical timing has its structural impact: after all the bloody scenes, butchery, raving, mockery, and other unnatural acts, Henry invokes the pastoral life, orderly, quiet, natural, fecund. Against this lament – ironic in Henry's abdication of the responsibility of his kingly office of shepherding his subjects – the Son–Father scene becomes that much more brutal in its abstraction. Formal, choral, almost liturgical in its lamentation, it externalizes his burdens of conscience while emotionally invoking standards of order denied by the rest of the play. Brought back to the atrocities of civil war for which he must take responsibility, Henry realizes at the end of the scene that he can do nothing to change those realities. At this point in the 1977 RSC production directed by Trevor Nunn, Alan Howard as Henry "makes Henry impossibly slow to move, even having difficulty speaking Exeter's name, and rising with the crown in his hand, putting it swiftly on Margaret's head on his last lines, and then, actually ahead of them, calling both ironically and as from a great mental distance, 'Forward 'a-way!'"

One could elaborate upon the theatrical effectiveness of the scene: the theatergoer, for example, would more readily make the connection that Henry sits down upon the same stage molehill on which York was taunted with the paper crown and savagely executed by Margaret and Clifford (I.4). If in reading the scene appears archaic, crude, and stylistically inappropriate, Barry Jackson's sense of theater reminds us to attend to the audience's response and Trevor Nunn's stage business reinforces visually Henry's combination of sensibility and escapism.

In short, the bits and pieces of such accounts as well as the more extensive reviews and reconstructions of performances will constantly send us back to the printed text to verify, reexamine, dispute, and shrug our shoulders. The winds of history blow fair and foul. In the late 1950s producing *Henry V* as straight epic became increasingly more problematic: the virile, romantic hero – Olivier's performance in the 1944 film has stamped this interpretation permanently in our consciousness – would not play to an audience disillusioned with the glories of war, national, just, or otherwise. Though a sense of the play's ironies dates at least as far back as the years immediately after World War I, no one dared to stage a non-charismatic Henry until Peter Hall's 1964 RSC production. Gareth Lloyd Evans' response indicates the distance from Olivier's version: "The heroism, where it exists, is found almost entirely in sheer dogged pugnaciousness. It is the heroism of the First World War trenches, of attrition, of unsung deeds done as a matter of course, and of men following a leader, not because he is a king, but because he is as tired and as stubbornly determined as they are."[10] In 1975 Terry Hands directed Alan Howard as a morally queasy Henry, scrupulously reluctant and full of self-doubt, in an attempt to "square anti-militarist scruples with a full-blooded treatment of the great national folk tale."[11] If these recent productions remind us that performance as interpretation depends upon directors' expectations of audience response, they also send us to the printed text again to read its theatrical dimensions from a new perspective, perhaps even convincing some die-hard followers of the straight epic interpretation that the ironies of *Henry V* are indeed actable.

Another area in which stage history can usefully help our reading of Shakespeare's dramaturgical intentions lies in the surgical operations performed in production. Not always are the omissions in performances dictated by the necessity to cut the text to the two-and-a-half hours' traffic of the modern stage. The Aumerle scenes in *Richard II* provide an instructive example. Often entirely cut, the scene of the gages which forms a prologue to Richard's deposition (IV.1) and Aumerele's desperate pleading with Bolingbroke (V.3) verge upon farce. Arthur Colby Spragrue and J. C. Trewin comment that

the successive rush of son, father, and mother into Bolingbroke's presence . . . must nearly always start a laugh from the audience, just as the throwing-down of the gages does in Westminster Hall . . . . A director cannot allow the gages to mount up. The text calls for seven throws; towards the end, as noble upon noble joins in, the cumulative effect can be absurd. Anthony Quayle avoided this at Stratford [1951] by confining the throws to three, as many as the average audience will accept.[12]

Here again, directorial expectation governs the production, though at the level of scene rather than whole; the difference nevertheless prompts us who trust the text (and its "playability") and to re-examine these seldom-commented-upon scenes: did Shakespeare intend farce and why?

Shakespeare's sensitivity to audience responses should, of course, be questioned along with everything else, but most often his adeptness proves itself. Richard David, in objecting to another reviewer's squeamishness about the 1976 RSC's "overemphasis" upon Gloucester's blinding, asks: "What does he think Shakespeare was doing, if not going all out, as in the scene of the murder of the Macduffs, to secure a gut-revulsion in the audience."[13] The director must trust Shakespeare since, as Barry Jackson notes in discussing the opening scene of *3 Henry VI*, in which Richard Crookback throws down Somerset's severed head, the line "between the risible and the serious is of such infinitesimal breadth that the reaction of the audience can never be foretold."[14] In a similar situation, James Sandoe in producing *2 Henry VI* (for the Oregon Shakespeare Festival in 1954) wondered about the reaction of the audience to the Jack Cade scenes and discovered their effectiveness when his audiences found their laughter turning sour as the farce turned grotesquely savage.[15]

These observations are not meant to demonstrate beyond doubt Shakespeare's dramatic artistry in the history plays; the following chapters, in part, attempt that. They are meant to suggest some of the problematic areas of interpreting the aspects of the per-formance (not the specific elements of particular productions) of Shakespeare's texts. All the examples in this section have involved the responses of an audience to scenes or to central characters. In helping us to re-think the ways in which Shakespeare's dramatic techniques actually work in the theater, the materials of stage history cannot lead us astray if they send us down new routes in our return to the text.

THEATRICALITY AND POLITICS

Seeing the history plays as plays, then, involves the paradox that the visual, aural, and kinesic elements of performance are both absent from and present within the printed pages the interpreter shuffles in his study. Equally absent yet present are two other aspects of theater which require consideration: the theatricality of Elizabethan culture and the theater as an institution within that culture. If stage conventions, staging practices, and other factors in the physical conditions of production and in the theatrical dimensions of dramatic texts can sometimes be recovered and enfolded into the annotation of act, scene, and line without always radically altering critical "readings," placing the texts and their theater within history – as opposed to or in addition to filling the editions of texts with history – often opens new possibilities of locating the plays within the social circumstances and the historical moment of the larger cultural matrix.[16] In turn, such critical procedures collapse the security of an historical background from which the foreground of literary analysis advances to the apron of critical consciousness; by ignoring the traditional emphasis upon the singularity of artistic production and the autonomy (narrowly defined) of the text, they reveal the implication of the text in its society and history and also the presence of the culture in the dramatic text, a presence often but dimly perceived because these apparently extratextual "facts" belong to the shadows of gloss, footnote, and mechanical handbook literary history. Considered together, these various aspects of Elizabethan theatricality reciprocally inform each other and repay our efforts to make the connections of stage and society by intensifying the power of the reversible formula: All the world's a stage. Read forward and backward, the equation discloses the political dimension of Elizabethan theater, especially of drama portraying English kings, and its potential for promoting or subverting the dominant ideology of its immediate culture.[17]

The Elizabethans themselves never doubted that all history is contemporary history: the value of history exists in its practical utility as a teacher of religious, ethical, and administrative lessons.[18] Neither has twentieth-century criticism ignored the reflection of Elizabethan concerns in Shakespeare's history plays: Tillyard placed them within the framework of his Elizabethan

World Picture, and Lily B. Campbell's analysis of them as "mirrors of Elizabethan policy" complemented his work.[19]
While each saw Shakespeare transcending as well as reflecting the broadest and narrowest concerns of the period from 1585 to 1595, both presented a case for an orthodox, rather rigid ideological scheme of things at the cosmological and monarchical level which permitted little variation or dissent, little that could be considered polyphonic or problematic.[20] These studies from the 1940s established the critical framework for several decades, and although now much of the security of such a monological vision has been effectively challenged as too reductive and limiting, the presence of the providential view and its accompanying corollaries in Shakespeare is undeniable. Reputable literary historians are still providing us with the straight Tillyard sense of order and Shakespeare's terror of the chaos of rebellion.[21] Others, fortunately, have recognized the complexity of Elizabethan power, ideology, and subversion and the problems of accepting a literary approach in which the text frequently but innocently reflects the assumptions of its culture.[22] The connections among a play's theatricality, the culture's theatricality, and the theater's theatricality help to illuminate the problematic nature of the history plays' history, to see its contemporaneity in all its facets and to assess its representation of the ideological issues its original audiences would have been aware of but which are hidden from today's readers.[23]

Recent historians of Elizabeth I's reign also are questioning received opinions of the Virgin Queen's greatness and the achievements of England during the last half of the sixteenth century.[24] The portrait drawn by William Camden's *Annales* in the 1620s established the agenda for historians until very recently, and like Tillyard's providential order, the presence of a dominant, dynamic, and effective Elizabeth is both true and monological. The golden age of unity and prosperity was accepted in both popular and scholarly accounts and seemed unshakeable, especially after Sir John Neale's magisterial volumes; undoubtedly, stability, felicity, certainty, and cohesiveness characterize Elizabeth's long rule and justify her praises among Elizabethans and moderns; what has become clearer in the last few decades is that heterogeneity, local independence, division, and disruption demand a place in the presentation of Elizabethan culture.[25] Power must be treated as more problematic, history as more polyphonic. If an historian's re-synthesis of Elizabethan culture seems far off, as unavailable

now as does a literary scholar's, the current research at least
indicates the probability that some of the Elizabethans themselves
saw through the ruses of the dominant ideology, the asymmetries
in the allocation of resources, the impressive displays of highly
theatrical myths of order and greatness, the everyday failures of
the nation to function as the monarch pretended it did.

The theatricality of the last two decades of Elizabeth's reign may
be seen as extending and transforming the Tudor Myth. Tillyard
identified two of Henry VII's strategies for bolstering the legitimacy
of his title: that his union of the houses of York and Lancaster was
the providential conclusion to the anarchic Wars of the Roses and
that through his Welsh ancestry his claim to the throne was inde-
pendent of both Lancastrian and Yorkist descent and would usher
in a return of the golden age of Arthur whose qualities of leadership
he had inherited from Cadwaller.[26] Each of these strategies led to
a complex of iconographic and theatrical themes embodied in the
display of dynastic glory. As background for Shakespeare's history
plays, the Tudor Myth offers less an explanation than a rich source
of themes and images. Nowhere does Shakespeare present the myth
without seriously compromising the character who voices it, with
the possible exception of Richmond himself, who is hardly more
than an emblematic savior in *Richard III*, and none of the history
plays, with the partial exception of *Henry V*, promotes the ideology
of monarchical absolutism insisted upon by Elizabeth.

What is incomplete about Tillyard's Tudor Myth is its omission
of the problematic recreation of ideology by the Tudors. Henry
VII seized the opportunity of reordering the monarchy after the
Battle of Bosworth by asserting his control over the aristocracy,
turning semi-independent feudal lords into peers of the realm
and making them agents of royal authority rather than privileged heads of elaborate systems of vassalage. With so many
of the old nobility eliminated by the Wars of the Roses, he had
an easier task – only eighteen barons were called to his first
parliament – one accomplished by the effective use of the common law and the courts and by the manipulation of various
symbolic actions. It involved establishing his supremacy through
the enforcement of the inherited hierarchy, making it a reality,
and not by crushing the barons nor by creating new institutions of government: the nobles simply became servants of the
state.[27] This achievement forms the lasting triumph of Henry
VII's administration and the foundation for the political ideology

and social theory that prevailed through the Tudor and into the Stuart dynasty.

The frontispiece to the 1536 Coverdale Bible (Figure 1) illustrates Henry VIII's interpretation of the monarchical hierarchy and expresses the transformatory nature of kingship, now augmented by the break with Rome. Holbein's title page lays out the architecture quite simply: seated on his throne below the title, Henry holds in his right hand the sword of justice and with his left delivers this Bible to his bishops. They kneel to one side and the nobles to the other, both obedient to the king whom the "Dedication" calls "in this world present the person of God . . . he only under God is the chief head of al the congregation and church of the same." Just above the kneeling bishops, the priests read Moses' Laws to their parishioners, and just above them is presented the scene of Moses' receiving the tablets on Mount Sinai. On the opposite side, above the nobles the lay aristocrats urge the people to spread the gospel, an injunction they imitate from Christ's sending his apostles into all the world, the image the panel just above them portrays. Above the title the top two narratives present Adam, Eve, and the Fall on the left and the Risen Christ on the right, giving the reader the dual justification of law and gospel, Old and New Testament, man's fallen nature and the redemption from sin and death through Christ's sacrifice. Between the two is the sun, emblem of God as the source of all.

Seen as an expression of the politics of the English Reformation, the 1536 title page reveals the underscoring of royal authority, the union of Church and State and the liberation of the English monarch from deference to Rome. But it also strikingly displaces the nobility to a position of subservience by making them servants of the single source of rule. Visually, Henry has wrested control from both the Pope's bishops and from the barons and has re-created them as instruments of the monarch. The effectiveness of the image may be partly measured by the further displacement of religious images by emblems of royal authority in church and cathedral as well as by the dissolution of the monasteries and the reallocation of ecclesiastical property to the crown.

Holbein's title page provides us with a model of the Tudor ideology of a single source of authority, a vertical hierarchy of autonomy and dependence, and a benevolent view of the monarch's using the resources at his disposal to transform his subjects and in so doing both validate and extend his dominance. In turn, this

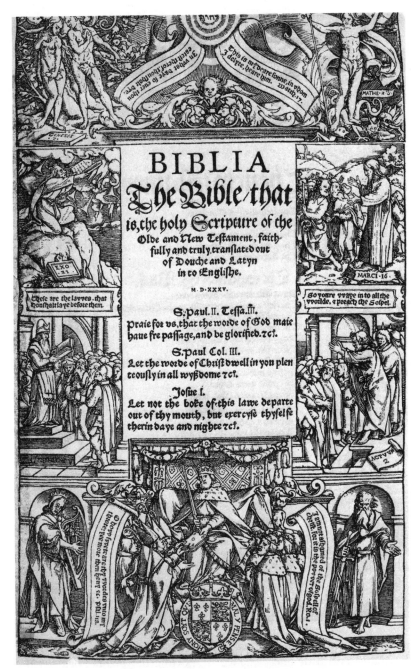

Figure 1   Title page of the Coverdale Bible, 1635. *Mansell Collection*

process is reproduced at lower levels by the faithful transmission of this benevolent transformation by the clergy and the aristocracy. If the example in this model is the Holy Bible, it could just as well be other resources – the institutions of the law, education, the court, culture – except that the scriptures more easily lend themselves to a secure display of authority and its ideology. The monarch employs the structural components of the system he has inherited and reorganizes them to maintain the order and stability of the realm, to augment its prosperity and encourage the religiosity, civic virtue, patriotism, and education of its citizens; such is the theory behind the Tudor Myth: dominant ideology at the monarchical level through resources at the institutional level – church and nobility – brings about transformation at the level of human agency.[28] Power is expressed in the process, in the instantiation of resources: here the extraordinary event – the translation of the Bible into the vernacular – retains its momentousness and ideological value as an instantiation of Reformation politics, but becomes by the reproduction of the moment down through the hierarchy a daily, routine procedure, thus extending the relational nature of power by means of the monarch's servants and thereby strengthening the dominant ideology. Power, then, is relational, and ideology is the justification, legitimization, glorification, and whatever other processes go into creating, sustaining, sanctioning, and improving the relations of power.

The title page of the Tyndale or Great Bible of 1539 (Figure 2) makes the ideology of the Tudor monarch even clearer and simpler by placing Henry VIII below God as before, but now the bishops and nobles both receive the *"verbum dei"* as they kneel and in turn they pass on the new Bible to the people, who fill up the space below them and respond by crying out *"vivat rex"* or "God save the king," the shout of those obviously lower in the social hierarchy. The arrangement states the divinity of the monarch and his role in bringing his subjects the Word of God, and emphatically it is the king who deserves the praise. The benevolence and largesse are repeated by the institutional representatives of church and nobility who strengthen the rhetoric of the model by asserting their eager service to its ideology. In Elizabeth's variation on this Tudor iconography – the title page for the 1569 Bishops' Bible (Figure 3) – the monarch enthroned is accompanied by the four daughters of God, Justice and Mercy holding a coronet above her head and Fortitude and Patience supporting her throne. Below her

Figure 2 Title page of the Great Bible, 1539. *Mansell Collection*

are many noblemen listening to several bishops, the whole group detached from the queen. The people are not represented. Though these changes may be significant, they need not detain us here: the main point is that the single source ideology of monarchical authority is reproduced by Elizabeth.

The model goes beyond visual rhetoric, although such iconographical display is clearly itself an example of the model at work: the title page as a resource for the expression of power as a relational concept in which the subjects are transformed and enfolded into the ideological unity of the realm. It goes beyond rhetoric because the Tudors, and Elizabeth especially, thought in terms of this process of structuration. Elizabeth's reign, then, may become benevolent and utopian or despotic and oppressive depending upon whether the Elizabethan citizen or the modern scholar concentrates upon the positive sanctions involved (rewards, inducements, influence) or the negative (punishments, threats, coercion). Some recent scholars have preferred the latter, reconstituting an Elizabethan Age of absolutism, with power concentrated in the hands of a very few who systematically "demonized" the unconforming, deviant, and poor and ruthlessly eliminated them or oppressed them through severe poverty and other punitive measures including surveillance, imprisonment, taxes, fines, and social stigmatization.[29] In other words, the ideological system worked well, but the transformations produced a government which could be described as golden only in the rhetoric of the ruling fraction not in the lived experience of the age. To some extent, of course, they are correct, and many examples of "demonizing" can be provided: they form scenes on the stage of Tudor politics.

One of the most theatrical and revealing of these involved the case of the ironically named John Stubbs, who had in 1579 published a polemical treatise opposing Elizabeth's proposed marriage to the Duke of Anjou.[30] Though his arguments were shrewd and well presented, though they had been presented in a very similar form in Council, though Stubbs was himself well connected, and though, of course, the marriage was not to be, Elizabeth reacted in anger and ordered all copies destroyed. Stubbs and his bookseller lost their right hands to the cleaver for interfering with Elizabeth's diplomacy; Stubbs's loyalty to Protestant politics (Anjou was Catholic) and his national pride (no marriage was necessary, a position Elizabeth had followed for twenty years) gained this brutal and public penalty, executed upon the scaffold in the marketplace at

Figure 3 Queen Elizabeth attended by the Daughters of God. *Bishop's Bible* (London, 1569). *Mansell Collection*

Westminster. Camden gives his own eyewitness account of Stubbs's putting on his hat with his left hand "so soon as his right hand was off" and crying "God save the queen." The multitude of onlookers were silent, "either out of an Horrour at this new and unwonted kind of Punishment, or else out of Commiseration towards the man, as being of an honest and unblameable Repute; or else out of Hatred of the Marriage, which most men presaged would be the Overthrow of Religion."[31] The law under which Stubbs and Page were tried dated from the time of Mary; the fury of the queen occasioned protest, and she countered by sending one lawyer to the Tower and by reprimanding one Justice of the Common Pleas so sharply that he resigned.[32] Yet later Sir Philip Sidney borrowed from Stubbs in criticizing the Anjou marriage and Stubbs himself would serve the government again in the 1580s.[33] The incident confirms the decisiveness and authority of Elizabeth, but also complicates our response, dividing it between "horror" and "commiseration" for Stubbs, the bookseller, the lawyer, and the justice and admiration for the queen's effective theatricalization of her royal will.

If, however, the Tudor ideology worked well enough to produce this and other occasions displaying the actuality behind the rhetoric of absolutism, it also worked well to promote a quiet and benevolent regime, worked in other ways than it presented itself as working, and often worked not at all. The pyramidal model of Tudor ideology, of the unitary conception of power, foundered upon the lack of institutional resources. In the recurrent operations of daily life, Elizabeth's policies suffered from the inadequacy of staffing legal and clerical offices and often were impossible to enforce in the face of indifference, disagreement, and social heterodoxy. She could call on neither a professional police force nor a standing militia to enforce her laws; their implementation depended upon the moral and social homogeneity and resources of local officials and their communities. Attempts to centralize the judicial institutions and to codify the penal laws often seem to be of more symbolic than real value, since unsympathetic localities were unwilling to enforce them, both because the punishments were too severe and because the codified handbook went against informal traditions of dealing with offenders.[34] Modifying and updating the penal code appears in large part to be rhetorical, a method of emphasizing the rightness of the queen's intentions and values and her expression of the Crown as the single source of institutional authority: she was trying to meet the needs of

England's communities. Of course, the quest for uniformity in all aspects of the nation's life had long since been a hallmark of Tudor administration, the means of underscoring the ideology the biblical title pages visualize.

Elizabeth's religious policies evidence the clearest area in which her desire for uniformity caused her problems. The 1559 Book of Common Prayer and Act of Uniformity attempted to fix the official version of the English Reformation, yet the Puritans could not be satisfied with the compromise. The government, acting benevolently to improve an inadequately educated clergy, in effect promoted opposition to the once-and-for-all Church of England Elizabeth always believed she had established. She cared mostly for the external conformity of her church, but would countenance very few genuine reforms during her reign, and, true to the Tudor model of governance, she regarded all suggestions of presbyterianism as insubordination: the bishops were instruments of service to the state. Edmund Grindal's refusal to order the suspension of local discussions of the Bible resulted in his suspension as Archbishop of Canterbury, and if his replacement, John Whitgift, was more effective in disbanding these reputedly "presbyterian cells," he did not silence the demands for reform.[35] Meanwhile, the variety of spirituality, conformity, and actual practice among the clergy belied the efforts at centrality and uniformity, the myth of transformation rhetorically insisted upon by the ideological model, and the loyalty of the clergy to the Crown. Elizabeth's lack of consistent interest in religious matters allowed her councillors to influence ecclesiastical appointments, and often they successfully urged upon her clergy at high rank who, if not overtly inimical to the Anglican Settlement, could hardly have been considered supporters. The favorite, Robert Dudley, Earl of Leicester, leader of the left-leaning Protestants and proponent of England's involvement in the politics of the Reformation on the international stage, advanced ecclesiastics of a like mind rather than served the queen's religious policy; whatever Leicester's ultimate loyalty to Elizabeth, he developed a wide clientage network which revealed the Tudor ideological system working in a rather non-pyramidal fashion.[36] Just how influential were Leicester and other Elizabethan nobles – court magnates and regional lords who maintained similar if less extensive systems of influence and clientage – may best be left to historians; the existence of factions and the continued importance of the nobility in determining the affairs of state appears certain, both to recent scholars and surely

to the Elizabethans who were constantly complaining about the
"backbiting" at Court.

That the Elizabethans were aware of contradictions between the
theory and practice of Tudor monarchy should be clear, even
without the hindsight of the Essex Rebellion or the abuses of the
Stuarts. Perhaps the growing interest in theatricality and myth-
making in the 1580s reflects anxiety and desperation as much as it
does confidence and pride. Elizabeth had passed her child-bearing
years, and after Anjou marriage appeared unlikely; her refusal to
discuss the succession worried many of her councillors and nobles.
The chivalry of the Accession Day tilts and tournaments dates from
around 1580, and the myths of Astraea, Gloriana, and the Virgin
Queen become more widespread soon after that. The curious affair
of "the Association" put together in 1584 to protect her against the
threat of assassination shows the aristocrats' sidestepping the usual
mechanisms of the Tudor state and turning to their own resources.[37]
Leicester's accepting the governor-generalship of the Netherlands
in 1586 was squelched by Elizabeth's asserting her authority, but
Leicester's insubordination along with the loss of most of the
towns on the Continent his forces had taken could not but put
the government in a bad light. Anxiety about a Spanish invasion
was extreme in the years before the defeat of the Armada. Though
this great English victory boosted the Crown's glory, enough had
happened in the 1580s to evidence the fragility of the Tudor myth
and the cracks in its ideology.

If Elizabeth's exercise of personal rule was far less extensive than
her Stuart successors', she used her inner circle of favorites to
keep much of her policy-making secret and her royal courts to
execute her justice, occasioning satirical comment even from those
at Court and angering the lawyers and judges of the common
courts. Parliament, the forum for the aristocracy and gentry, was
bypassed at times and at others silenced – religious reform and
the question of succession, for example, could not be discussed
– and the nobles outside the exclusive inner circle complained
of the difficulty of gaining access to the Queen. Meanwhile, the
myth-making assumed the model of a single source of authority,
replacing the Deborah who had delivered the nation in 1558 with
every manner of goddess from classical mythology and asserting
Elizabeth's equality with her masculine European rivals in dynastic
glory. The imagery insisted upon the virgin Eliza enthroned in the
heavens supported by the daughters of God and upon her Council,

bishops, nobles, and Parliament insuring the unity, prosperity, and justice of the realm and thereby securing her royal authority; the realities of governance were that the Queen remained secluded with her personal counsellors except for well-chosen theatrical appearances which she orchestrated with the greatest of dramatic talent.[38] As long as things went smoothly, the provincial nobility were satisfied with their territorial dominance of daily life, the Privy Council with the implementation and management of policy, Parliament with the fine tuning of the laws. Elizabeth could enjoy her privacy and privileged visibility; to tear the veil from the many mythological faces of Elizabeth could be in the interest of no one.[39] It is not so much that her anger was feared, though the Stubbs case shows her volatility, but that demystifying Eliza could serve no useful purpose.

Elizabeth invented the resources through which she dominated her subjects, nobles and commoners alike. The summer progresses to the great houses of the provincial nobility cost her much less than entertaining at Court and established at least a theatrical relationship between London and the counties. The Accession Day festivities at Westminster created a secular holiday to replace the carnivalesque celebrations which the age's anti-catholicism was discouraging. Her incarnations as Diana, Cynthia, Angelica, Gloriana, Astraea, Britannia, and the Virgin Queen cost her nothing and won her the praises of poets and citizens alike. The rhetoric of monarchy used all the arts of display to present the Queen as the only actress on the stage of politics.[40] The populace were engaged as spectators, invited to admire their goddess from a distance which precluded participation, even by those able and interested in playing a role in the governance of the nation, those aristocrats and gentry scrambling for preferment, place, and patronage or merely sitting faithfully in Parliament. As almost every portrait of Elizabethan noblemen illustrates, the outer circles of the Court were theatricalized by the revival of chivalry, the acculturation of European conventions of courtly behavior, and the prevalence of Petrarchan politics, that is, the translation of attendance at Court into erotic metaphors of serving an unattainable mistress. None of Elizabeth's politics as theater contradicts the usual popular image of Elizabeth Regina, but it does suggest the vulnerability of the mythology in which she surrounded herself. Her admirers marvelled at her skills in performance, and she herself admitted the pride of an actress on many occasions. "We princes are set on stages in the sight and view of all the world duly observed,"[41] she told the Lords and Commons in 1586, and she took an obvious delight in playing her audiences, according to her nephew, Sir John Harington, to Francis Bacon, and to many other observers. She imposed her fictions upon the Court, while pretending to accept their imposition upon her, and this theatrical passivity became another of the fictions she fostered. Elizabeth's encouraging poets and playwrights as well as courtiers to woo her had the effect of discouraging demarcations between literary and political discourse, and, to a great extent, her aestheticizing politics had the inevitable consequences of politicizing aesthetics and of extending the latitude for the play and interpretation of images whose force as ideological persuasion had long been declining. Indeed, while the pastoral and Petrarchan politics of Elizabeth's court supplemented the Tudor theory of monarchy, they also tended to overshadow such archaic legitimizations by creating a language of myth and fantasy whose pleasures as aesthetic play and entertainment outweighted its power as political authority.

Elizabeth's vanity, cleverness, and political style will not evoke negative responses and probably will augment the admiration of modern scholars. But it must be realized that there existed clearly apparent discrepancies between the Tudor ideology and the realities of political governance on the one hand and the lived experience of daily life on the other. Second, the fictions the Queen and her followers had encouraged became so exaggerated in their mythological multiplications and so discordant with the facts of an aging Elizabeth in the 1580s and 1590s that they must have become transparent propaganda to many observers. Third, the Queen's favoring – or perhaps because of the scarcity of institutional resources desperately resorting to – theatrical politics illustrates that the Elizabethan stage was not alone in insisting upon the *theatrum mundi* metaphor and that the average theatergoer who saw an English history play by Shakespeare would have assumed that all history is contemporary history, just as Elizabeth did when she exclaimed: "I am Richard II. Know ye not that?" Elizabeth had helped to construct the conventions of the stage of politics, though its basic nature had been conceived by the first Tudor and long ago had been laid bare by Thomas More, who equated at least some "king's games" with "stage plays."[42]

THE THEATER AS AN INSTITUTION

Patronage and "licensing" were the carrot and stick with which Elizabeth attempted to control the players as well as the printers; though the outlines of the growth of a professional theater in London during the last thirty years of the sixteenth century have often been clearly delineated, the ironies and complexities of its political status have not always been appreciated. On more than one occasion, Elizabeth saved the London stages from the annihilation their opponents seemed on the verge of achieving, yet from several perspectives her defense of the theater could hardly have been in her best interest, however effectively and restrictively the Master of the Revels or the Court of Ecclesiastical Commission might censor the plays to be performed. From the very beginning of her reign, the Queen had rightly interpreted her father's break with Rome to mean that under the Tudor ideology all religious questions were questions of national politics and vice versa; in short, if the monarch were the single source of authority, she was also the single source of the Word, of all words. Under the previous Tudors and during the early part of her reign, attempts to regulate and to suppress the players and the press had been sporadic and disorganized, but in the 1570s and 1580s the government through legal proclamations and improvements in the institutional bureaucracy aggressively used its influence to enforce the royal prerogatives to intervene in matters of the theater by concentrating more and more authority in the Office of the Revels and its director, the Lord Chamberlain.[43] Concurrently, the informal institutions of patronage presented poets and playwrights with positive inducements rather than negative sanctions, promoting the celebration of Elizabeth and her nation more effectively, despite the inconsistencies of the Queen in dispensing favors and rewards.[44]

Within these general contexts of State censorship and Court patronage, the professional theater of Shakespeare's time developed as an institution of Elizabethan culture and generated both its capacity for pleasing the Queen and its potential for subverting the pyramidal structure of monarchy and its hierarchical ideology. The patent granted to Leicester in 1574, in fact, justified the public performances of his company of players on weekdays in London as rehearsals for their playing before the Court; the theater had legally been placed under the indirect patronage of the Queen and its professionals made her servants. Such a gesture of royal approbation and encouragement influenced the aristocratic support for a favored form of recreational leisure and the entrepreneurial interest of commercial speculators who quickly seized the opportunity for fostering a burgeoning new industry, thus providing the theater with allies it would desperately need in fighting off the opposition not only of the Puritan outrage at the immorality of the drama itself and its competition for the popular audience, but also of the metropolitan authorities whose business it was to insure a decent and reasonable standard of order and public health and of the mercantile class whose apprentices might forego a sermon but not a play and spend their afternoons away from their appointed tasks.

The story of this hostility has too frequently been described as the Puritan attack on the stage; especially after 1576 – the date of the building of The Theatre – the permanent theaters attracted prostitutes and thieves, occasioned riots, caused traffic problems, and offered a breeding ground for contagious disease. They disrupted the lives of the citizen and merchant as well as the religious life of the community. The same, however, could be said of other cultural diversions which attracted large numbers of the populace and were placed in the disreputable suburbs of London. The potential of the theater for disruption, however, went beyond its ability to draw crowds; the physical conditions of seeing and hearing a play are themselves potentially subversive.

Based as it is upon illusion and pretence, the drama represents the truth through fictions whose formalizations obscure but cannot hide the duplicity of its metaphors. The permanent theater created a new kind of cultural space in which the very act of "playing" confused the everyday certainties of the social order. The clarity and opacity of the social life the theatergoer thought he had left behind him for the two-hours' traffic of the stage are exposed in the theatricality of dramatic presentation; at least Stephen Gosson was confused:

> In Stage Playes for a boy to put on the attyre, the gesture, the passions of a woman; for a meane person to take upon him the title of a Prince with counterfeit porte, and traine, is by outwarde signes to shewe them selves otherwise then they are, and so within the compasse of a lye . . . . We are commanded by God to abide in the same calling wherein we are called, which

is our ordinary calling in a commonweale . . . . If privat men be suffered to forsake theire calling because they desire to walke gentlemen like in sattine & velvet, with a buckler at theire heeles, proportion is so broken, unitie dissolved, harmony confounded, that the whole body must be dismembred and the prince or the heade cannot chuse but sicken.[45]

Though Gosson's primary intention may be to deny the "player" the status of a professional, he clearly objects to the duplication of the social realm in the theater by those who pretend to be what they are not. The stage presentation offers the audience a threateningly opaque view of reality – things may not be as they seem: boys may appear as women and commoners as kings – and simultaneously a threateningly clear view of the theatrical nature of social life beyond the confines of the auditorium: the hierarchical arrangements of the "commonweale" may be dependent solely upon "outwarde signes," the clothing and gestures of the nobleman but the visible manipulations of a deceptively healthy culture. Even to suggest such possibilities proved the public theater an abomination, a subverter of order. Because the actors were so proficient in replicating the world outside the theater, they challenged its presuppositions about the naturalness of social stratification. However scholars may quarrel over the "realism" of Elizabethan styles of acting, the players did consciously imitate their social betters in costuming, spending as much and more upon the finery of nobility as they did upon securing playscripts, and apparently this aspect of the spectacle comprised an important element of the theater's ability to draw in the populace.

Gosson's remarks accurately describe the magic of dramatic illusion: theater cannot but reflect contemporary social norms of dress and behavior and cannot but present reality as theatrical and dramatistic: the stage is all the world. Such an anti-theatrical perspective also rests upon the radical distrust of the visual, common in the post-Reformation fear of image and ritual as a deceptive displacement of the divinely inspired word.[46] Pretence could have no godly place in the commonwealth, and the players in wearing the cast-off robes of the aristocracy and vestments of the Church must have presented very convincing imitations of their social betters.[47] By its very nature, the theater exposed the theatricality of its culture and the visible politics of its royal and aristocratic patrons.

The correspondence in visible appearances blurred Gosson's sense of the boundaries between the fictional world of the play and the real world of society, and the collapse of distinctions in the mimetic "playing" subverted categories. The earlier drama had been anchored in certainties of relationship and therefore meaning, the authority of the Scriptures for the mystery plays, the simple allegorical identifications of the morality interludes, but Elizabeth had suppressed the religious stage, and the simplistic personifications and extreme contrasts of the moralities proved too wearisome for sophisticated audiences. With the loss of an instructionally motivated script, interpretation became problematic; without the security of pre-existent stories and meanings, the public stage allowed a holiday escape into illusion.[48] The representational shorthand of costume, for example, evoked the mimetic identification of social types and called into stage existence the corresponding hierarchies to confound those as distrustful of fiction as Gosson. Like the carnivalesque popular festivals which the Puritan divines disliked equally as much if not more, the public theaters enacted a release from the everyday restrictions of business as usual. The public stage in its very nature brought into question the solidity of the social world's values, even if the content of its dramas upheld orthodox versions of the Tudor ideology. Spectators could enjoy the villainy of Sedycyon in a play like Bale's *King Johan*, but the seditious noblemen in the Henry VI plays, for instance, prompt less immediate equations of role and reality.[49] Moreover, the kind of opposition Gosson may be taken to represent forced the theater to become more self-conscious of its own medium, further compounding the problems of the magic of its illusions as it often made the carnivalesque and the theatrical a thematic matter and evolved a spectrum of self-reflexive techniques to insist upon its powers of pretence.[50]

If the subversive nature of the public theater as a cultural institution seems overstated, one has only to turn to the private stage of the 1580s for comparison. Here the intention of Lyly, Peele, and others was to blur the distinctions between play world and Court world by elevating the fictionality of each into the realm of allegory and personification, mythological parable, and intellectual debate. The praises of Elizabeth are sung in a courtly world of verbal wit, Platonic artifice, and Ovidian metamorphoses in Lyly's idealized offerings, and the theatrical illusion itself is deliberately and wonderfully broken at the end of *The Arraignment of Paris* when Diana steps into the audience to award the "ball of golde," symbol of all of virtues, of beauty, rule, and wisdom, into the hands of Queen Elizabeth herself. The boundary of play and court is erased by the fiction's inclusion of the monarch; drama incorporates itself within "the liturgy of State."[51] Lyly's adulatory portraits of Elizabeth in the idealized Cynthia, Sapho, and Queen of Lesbos similarly enfold the mythology of virgin queen and perfect monarch into a theatrical fantasy freed from the anxieties and vicissitudes of the Court.

Many modern readers have rightly been impressed by the artistic achievement of Peele's play and some of Lyly's allegories; they manipulate their symbolic resources with an elaborate gracefulness and reach for a high level of lyricism and rhetorical sophistication. But their success in dissolving the boundary of myth and court or in transforming the theater's arts of illusion into worshipful rituals cannot efface the nature of the medium. Almost all the plays which extravagantly promoted the mythology of the Virgin Queen were written for the private theaters or the Court and were performed by companies of boy actors. However highly textured the language and complex the shows, the display of this familiar mythology to an audience of aristocrats only momentarily gathers them into its magic, for the staging of ideology – as opposed to its discursive expression – discloses the procedures whereby the illusions are created and so reveals the fictionality of the royal audience's attempts to translate the political into the courtly erotic. Within the real ambience of the Court, even those who admired Elizabeth's theatricality had to first see it as manipulation: wearing the mask of poetic myth may hide the face of politics but simultaneously reveals that a mask is being worn. Her own godson, Sir John Harrington, for instance, in writing about the Queen's subtlety in imposing her will, describes the inducements of personality and "sweet and refreshing" speech, but his choice of verbs makes us recognize the theatricality and coercion which are concurrently displayed in the exercise of graciousness:

> Herein did she show her wisdom fully: for who did choose to love her confidence; or who would withhold a show of love and obedience, when their Sovereign said it was their choice, and not her compulsion? Surely she did play well her tables to gain obedience thus without constraint: again, she could put forth

such alterations, when obedience was lacking, as left no doubts whose daughter she was.[52]

The paradox of ideology, in Elizabeth's age or ours, is that in presenting itself it also calls attention to its own artifices of presentation, and nowhere is this as apparent as in the theater.[53]

The Children of the Chapel and of St Paul's could not be accused by Gosson of subverting the social hierarchy by avoiding their normal vocation for that of the actor, since they were, after all, schoolboys, but the same disparity of role and reality also limits the effectiveness of the attempt to dissolve the boundaries of art and life, fiction and court. The Queen and her courtiers might receive the frenzied adulation of aspiring playwrights but from the voices and gestures of boys whose professionalism as actors, however proficient, could not efface the incongruity of visual appearance and ideological intent. The plays of Lyly and Peele performed at Court were, in a sense, antidramatic, and the audience which had commanded or at least fostered their creation enjoyed the pleasures of a festive celebration of its own community in proportion to the subordination of the theatrical to its own self-image.[54] Perhaps this fact – that the audience had really created the fictional world of the plays it attended – partially accounts for the paucity of rewards for Lyly, Peele, and the other designers of its praises; in any case, they were working against the medium for which they wrote, and without the willing complicity of the Court and aristocratic community in initiating and accepting their fictions, it is difficult to imagine them as theater at all. In establishing the affinities of play world and social world, the playwrights suppressed the distinctions between them but only by insisting upon the fictionality and theatricality of both: the underlying dramatistic world view of the stage again suggests the duality and paradoxes of the presentational celebration of the ideological community of the Court.

In contrast, without an audience whose shared values could be determined, without patrons and their limited circle of friends, Elizabethan dramatic poets writing for the public stage, especially Shakespeare, turned the *theatrum mundi* image inward, developing it within the play's fictions rather than unfolding the image outward and encouraging the theatrical culture to absorb it within its visible politics of self-display. The new audience for the new professional theater saw actors playing people consciously playing dramatic roles within the fictions, assuming disguises, parodying role prescriptions, deliberately deceiving other actors playing people, watching plays within plays, and so forth. No doubt, a primary motivation of the public theater's self-reflexiveness came from the novelty of the position in which the recently professionalized playwright found himself: he was asserting the efficacy of his craft's magical powers of illusion, both against the pressures of religious and municipal opposition and in affirmation of his skills and those of the players. Looked at from the public spectators' point of view, such complications of the theatrical metaphor as one finds, for example, in *Richard III*, might appear to create aesthetic distance between audience and play, and in some sense they do. But by thematizing the theatricality of the self, royal or otherwise, the play further insists upon the dramatistic interpretation of social reality, suggesting that the spectator face the theatricality of his own self-chosen role and thus occasioning involvement as well as alienation, sympathy for as well as reflection upon the poor players that Holofernes' group or Bottom's crew turn out to be in the early comedies.[55]

Whether or not such intricacies of self-reflexivity are intended to subvert Elizabeth social and political orthodoxies cannot always be ascertained by modern readers, but clearly the dramatistic metaphor fascinated Shakespeare and is inseparable from his theater; it leads to the brinksmanship of presenting the co-existence of the play's reality and unreality, the magic of illusion and the pretence of fiction and requires a multiple consciousness of its spectators much more complex than the perception of the enactment of figures from sacred history or the representation of intellectual abstraction. This reflexiveness is in itself *display*, a self-assertion central to the public theater's definition of its art and of whatever independence it could claim within the matrix of London culture, and central to its institutional integrity. The tenuousness of this integrity, in turn, meant a constant awareness of its nature as an institution, threatened as it was by opposition, suspension of activity, and extinction on one hand and by entrepreneurial cooptation, municipal regulation, state censorship, and ideological incorporation on the other. "At any moment," Glynne Wickham writes of the "bleak future" the professional theater might envisage for itself around 1592, "the stage could find itself at the centre of a political battleground as bitter and as bloody as the religious battlefield from which it had so narrowly escaped."[56] Harried by a culture in which everything was political, the public theater as an institution could hardly avoid politics nor could its plays avoid implicating that culture in its fictions, even those as apparently innocent as, for example, Shakespeare's early pastoral comedies.

By presenting a dramatistic, axiological, and primary mimetic world view, the public stage offered a completely different interpretation of social reality than the symbolic, hierarchical, ideologically rigid world view of the official culture. Introducing the characters of history onto the boards adds another element of subversion, because drama essentially relies upon the progressive unfolding of a story and history plays cannot avoid the subordination of the iconic present to the historic sequence. The courtly aesthetic – whether it displays itself in Lyly's comedies, Elizabeth's theatricality, or Hilliard's miniatures – strives for the timeless presence of the iconic and submerges experience in the patterns of the idea. The title pages of the previous section clearly illustrate the stasis of the iconic escape from the time-bound, but the stage insists upon its linear and dynamic nature, and playwrights like Lyly who emphasize the iconic transcendence of historic time struggle against the medium in which they work.[57] Elizabeth's great success partly depended upon her appropriation of history as well as myth: sacred history in her role as Deborah, the national deliveress; chivalric history in the panoply of tournaments and Accession Day tilts; English history in the continued refinements of the dynastic mythology; Ovidian history in the images of Cynthia or Astraea. All look toward fixing time in the iconic present and thereby controlling meaning: Spenser's narrative of Arthur's search for Gloriana perhaps most radically illustrates the disruption of history and its subordination to the iconic. Even in the early attempts at the "chronicle play," the influence of the static politics of the interlude leads to the dramatization of pre-existent morality and meanings: from John Bale's *King Johan* to *The Famous Victories of Henry the Fifth* the techniques of the iconic may change from morality play personifications to a sequence of illustrative episodes tenuously tied together, but seldom do such plays successfully overcome the difficulties of the stage's natural resistence to the transformation of history into iconography. The iconic, of course, remains essential in Shakespeare's history plays, but takes its subordinate place in the theatrical dialectic of idea and experience. In the early histories he was clearly searching for the proper uses of the static, emblematic scene: that of the Sons and the Fathers in *2 Henry VI* indicates the thematic value of the iconic and its theatrical potential when subordinated within the larger time-bound framework.

The theater itself, then, is potentially subversive in its very different orientation toward time, since one recurrent use of the iconic by ideology is to mystify the historic. The absolute monarch appropriates the historic and the right to assign it meanings, and Elizabeth clearly enjoyed imposing her fictions upon her subjects and jealously guarded her prerogatives in making policy.[58] If the theater by nature stops short of becoming institutionally committed to dismantling the symbolic constructs of ideology, it does present a very different aesthetic which competes with the ideological. As I hope I have made clear, the opposition of aesthetics – royal and courtly versus public stage – cannot be divorced from the opposition of values and methods of creating meaning. Even an historical play drawn from the Roman past such as *Julius Caesar*, written during the same period as the mature English history plays, exposes the mystifications of absolute sovereignty, as, for example, Cassius challenges the mythology of "Caesar" as the infallible interpreter of Rome's destiny.[59]

Both Tudor ideology and professional theater were products of the same highly stylized and formalized culture which tended to translate the political into the aesthetic. In the impossibility of not re-presenting the historical dramatistically, the stage internalized the ideological and revealed its theatricality, demystified its dictation of the tropes of the iconic, and opposed the flexibility of experience to the fixity of interpretation. The subversiveness of the theater as an institution may be overstated, but in a culture in which politics is seen as involving the arts of performance, plays which touch upon the history of English politics will not escape the implicit nature of the medium.

Like the carnivalesque entertainments which suspended or inverted the normal social world, the pleasures of an afternoon at the theater surely acted as a steam-valve for many Londoners. The two-hours' traffic of the stage was marked off from daily experience as clearly as were Shrovetide and Midsummer's Eve, and each was fundamentally entertainment. Neither popular festivity nor public theater promoted the revolutionary action which their forms dramatize within their demarcated temporal limits; the first simply turned the world upside down for a day without challenging the verticality of order, rank, wealth, and other usual forms of hierarchy; the second provided a site upon which the anxiety of contesting interpretations of social reality – the symbolic and the dramatistic

– could be played out. Back on the business-as-usual streets of London, the theatergoer had, however, absorbed the imaginative experience of a holiday from the normal structures of the official culture and perhaps even some of the cognitive perspective which insisted upon his seeing his society's theatricality and its fictions dramatistically.

Not all Elizabethan politics, of course, is monarchical politics, but concentration upon the Queen and Court illustrates readily the split in the last quarter of sixteenth-century England between the pride in achieving an aesthetically pleasing and convincing performance, in manipulating and imposing fictions, and the necessity of maintaining their reality as part of natural and immutable political order, in short between the flexibility of aesthetics and the fixity of ideology. The public theater provided the inevitable stage for politics.

2

Henry VI, Part One

SPECTACLES OF CHAOS

Even before *1 Henry VI* begins, Shakespeare uses the magic of the theater to establish an atmosphere of tragic solemnity and expectation: the spectator upon entering the auditorium would have seen the "heavens" and possibly some of the rest of the stage draped in black, perhaps "mournful streamers" fixed to the pillars as they were for Zenocrate's funeral in *2 Tamburlaine*, III.2. Curiosity about whose funeral is at hand has been evoked, and an ominous mood established in which the cosmic as well as the human level is involved. The solemn music of the "dead march," heralds bearing a wooden casket, and an ordered procession of mourners in black prolong the anticipation, as does the first speaker momentarily before he identifies the coffin's remains as those of the glorious Henry the Fifth (I.1.6). The first two as yet unidentified noblemen lament in speeches of symmetrical length, the first seeking the cause of the late king's untimely, premature death, the second praising his excellence as a warrior.

In its first minutes (the first sixteen lines), the play is appropriately ceremonial in solemnizing the great loss, yet the "bad revolting stars, That have consented unto Henry's death" and "Comets, importing change of times and states" suggest further disasters to come. The second speaker in taking up the image of "day into night" also intensifies the gloom and blackness ahead for England. If the average Elizabethan knew that Henry VI was still a child when he succeeded to the throne, the new king is nevertheless conspicuously absent, and his not appearing on stage until the beginning of the third act makes his eventual presence much more potentially dramatic. The typically Renaissance concern about the randomness of Fortune's animosity to human valor and aspiration has been introduced by the references to the unfavorable astrological configurations, and the mythic stature of a Marlovian superhero has been mourned in the hyberboles of the dead king's nonpareil feats.

The audience has been introduced to a fallen world, fallen heroically and historically – and as they soon learn fallen morally and theologically as well – by the lamentations of those we soon learn are the dead man's brothers. But from the formalities of the first two speeches, Exeter, the third speaker, redirects the ceremonious panegyrics by calling for action:

> We mourn in black: why mourn we not in blood?
> Henry is dead and never shall revive.
>   (17–18)

This realism cuts through the solemn mourning and questions the despair and its cause in the stars:

> What! shall we curse the planets of mishap
> That plotted thus our glory's overthrow?
> Or shall we think the subtle-witted French
> Conjurers and sorcerers, that, afraid of him,
> By magic verses have contriv'd his end?
>   (23–27)

The clergyman's intervention continues the praise of Henry V by identifiying him as "bless'd of the King of kings," but adds that "The Church's prayers made him so prosperous" (32). Now, the funeral ceremony degenerates into a brief squabble between this Bishop of Winchester and the aristocratic relatives of the deceased king, the latter accusing the Church of praying for his demise, refusing to support his wars in France, seeking power in the secular realm, and preferring the flesh to religion. The twin explanations in the play for the chaos of the present and the anarchy to come are first laid down here: the randomness of the stars and the devilish magic of the French. The possibility of God's intervention in history enters the discussion through the back door in the claim for and sarcastic response to the efficacy of prayer. Not only are the nobility and bishops jostling for power, but the audience also sees the relatively shallow confidence in the orthodox, providential dominance over historical event; astrology and sorcery appear to take precedence. Attempting to reconcile

Gloucester, whose wife the bishop accuses of pride, and Winchester, who wants to wrest power away from the regent and protector, Bedford plays the peace-maker, but while he prays for civil peace he expects trouble; his invocation of the ghost of Henry V to aid in the realm's prosperity, prevent "civil broils," and "combat with adverse planets in the heavens" (52–54) reintroduces the astrological at the expense of the theocratic and seems a desperate plea for the continued presence of Henry V. It is answered and interrupted by a sequence of messengers who announce progressively more disastrous events in France, together heralding the fulfilment of the fears that all that Henry V won might be lost. The solemn ceremony of the glorious Christian king's funeral has been twice broken: the squabbling of uncles and bishop undermines the sincerity of the laments and reveals the hollowness of the rhetorical prescriptions and ceremonial roles being fulfilled, and the three messengers with bad reports of English affairs in France emphasize the immediate vulnerability of military conquest, Henry V not yet buried before his successes are steadily being cancelled.[1] In a few moments the stately ceremony of state has given way to imminent despair and further loss, and visually and verbally the audience sees and hears that destruction as coming both from internal dissension and French aggression and from the contrary purposes of the stars and the black magic of the French. Although later Shakespeare acknowledges the official Tudor version of history – that all this chaos has come from the usurpation of Henry IV and the attendant curse of deposition and regicide (see II.5.63–72, for example) – the first scene seems deliberately uncircumscribed by any religious interpretation of history.

What might the Elizabethan spectator make of the opening scene? An orderly ceremony has given way to open hostility between the Protector and the bishop; the concern for the future well being of England has been unmasked as grasping for power; the glory of English conquest has been doomed even before its warrior-king has been laid to rest; the royal successor is notably absent; the Church seems to be set against the Crown. The first messenger becomes quite undeferential and openly upbraids the aristocrats for their lethargy – "Awake, awake, English nobility!" (78) – and the third and last messenger reports the imprisonment of Talbot, the great English general. The scene ends with a flurry of purposeful activity: Bedford will assemble a new army of ten thousand to fight in France; Gloucester will go to the Tower to examine the artillery and munitions and ready the proclamation of young Henry as king; Exeter will hasten to Eltham to safeguard young Henry. After symmetrical exits by these three, in the same order of their opening speeches, Winchester remains onstage to plot:

> Each hath his place and function to attend:
> I am left out; for me nothing remains;
> But long I will not be Jack out of office.
> The King from Eltham I intend to steal,
> And sit at chiefest stern of public weal.
>
> (173–77)

The couplet firmly rounds off the world of machinations into which the playwright has introduced his audience: stealing the public weal aptly describes the unceremonious scramble for power. The dramatic reversal from the solemnity of the ceremonial remembrances of Henry V to the self-serving soliloquy of the Bishop of Winchester points to the fragility of the orderly rituals of state and reveals the highly theatrical nature of politics.

The pattern of dramatic construction will be often repeated in the *Henry VI* plays, until the dignity and significance of the political and diplomatic "liturgy of state" becomes suspect in every regard. C. L. Barber's distinction here is helpful:

> The Renaissance . . . was a moment when educated men were modifying a ceremonial conception of human life to create a historical conception. The ceremonial view, which assumed that names and meanings are fixed and final, expressed experience as pageant and ritual – pageant where the right names could be changed in the right, the proper way. The historical view expresses life as drama. People in drama are not identical with their names, for they gain and lose their names, their status and meaning – and not by settled ritual: the gaining and losing of names, of meaning, is beyond the control of any set ritual experience.[2]

1 Henry VI from its opening scene becomes dramatic by exposing the gap between professed intention and true motive: the struggle for power between Gloucester and Winchester, Court and Church, threatens to displace the concern for the welfare of the nation. As the audience gradually learns who these figures in black are – giving "names" to characters – it also moves from the abstract anonymity of funereal mourning and eulogy to the specificity of the historical moment of losing French provinces. Bedford's onstage disrobing makes this movement visually theatrical:

> Regent I am of France:
> Give me my steeled coat: I'll fight for France.
> Away with these disgraceful wailing robes!
>
> (84–86)

Admirable as such determination is, even in an aging man, the immediate appearance of a second messenger with bad news interrupts his patriotism, just as the first messenger had broken off his prayer that the "ghost" of Henry V war against the "adverse planets" foreshadowing "civil broils" as well as renewed foreign wars (53–56). With the third messenger's entry, again an interruption of Bedford's mustering courage for the French wars, the cumulative theatrical effect stresses the uncontrollable in history, as Shakespeare models his opening scene after the Book of Job and draws together events from his chronicle sources which are spread over twenty-three years.[3] Though the English dominance did not begin to fall apart until seven years after Henry's death, the concentrated losses here underscore the sense of finality and international upheaval.

What the audience has seen is the ceremonial pageantry of royal funeral, dissension, messengers with progressively worse news, confusion, determination to act, and cynical scheming; all in the end foreboding wars with France. The scene hardly suggests the strengthened confidence of the English in the years immediately following the defeat of the Spanish Armada; the popularity of "Armada rhetoric" during the time of *1 Henry VI*'s composition would have seemed to ask for a play about Henry V not one which begins with his death and proceeds to dramatize English losses. (In a similar moment, Laurence Olivier found Shakespeare's *Henry V* appropriately patriotic for celebrating the heroic English victories of World War II.)[4] Instead, the presence of English forces on the continent, engaged in losing battles, points to the very recent history which falls upon either historical side of the Armada: the campaigns in the Low Countries from 1585 to 1587 and the military assistance of English troops on behalf of Henry of Navarre's claim to the French throne from 1590 to early 1592. Geoffrey Bullough

suggests that the play "would be topical at the end of 1591" and
that the audience would have associated its siege of Rouen (III.2–3)
with the Earl of Essex's forces' assisting the Huguenots' siege of
Rouen in the autumn of 1591.[5] The problems the English armies
encountered in their unsuccessful efforts to secure the French crown
for a Protestant claimant correspond closely to the first messenger's
very realistic response to Exeter's asking if Paris and Rouen had not
been lost through "treachery":

> No treachery, but want of men and money.
> Amongst the soldiers this is muttered –
> That here you maintain several factions:
> And whilst a field should be dispatch'd and fought,
> You are disputing of your generals;
> One would have lingering wars, with little cost;
> Another would fly swift, but wanteth wings;
> A third thinks, without expense at all,
> By guileful fair words peace may be obtain'd.
>   (69–77)

This analysis equally well describes the difficulties of the previous
campaigns in the Netherlands, with Elizabeth's vacillations, sending and calling home Leicester, withholding additional funds for
the expenses abroad; with Leicester's disputes with Sir John Norris,
Sir Thomas Wilkes, and others of his generals; with the dissension
among the Privy Councillors at home about foreign policy; with
the diplomatic negotiations after Leicester's resignation in 1587;
with the general "want of men and money." The messenger's
explanation provides a generic perspective upon the difficulties in
prosecuting a military strategy on continental soil, but one which
more accurately illuminates recent and contemporary internation-
alism and policy than that of the 1420s; within the play itself the
messenger's comment is not linked to any past history nor has it
warrant in any of the chroniclers, but it rather describes what we are
beginning to see in the present scene and will see more of later. Both
Leicester and Essex – his stepson, inheritor of his clientage network,
his chivalric self-image, and the cause of international Protestantism
– learned of such cruel limitations on the successful pursuit of their
military adventures.

Shakespeare saw the events of the past through the lenses of
recent history and appears to have deliberately implicated that

history in the affairs of Henry VI's reign. The reasons for this
topicality are not readily apparent from this first scene nor from
the entire play; however, locating *1 Henry VI* within the context of
contemporary adventures on the continent suggests some possible
approaches to Shakespeare's sense of the dual nature of the stage as
a site for dramatized interpretations of how history works as well
as of what happened and as an arena for the exploration of contemporary issues. The presence of the first messenger's appraisal opens
up an opposition between a provocatively realistic explanation
for the English failures in France and the superstitions of the
stars, sorcery, conjuration, and treachery. Blatantly un-romantic,
it implicitly undermines the high-minded chivalry of Leicester's
idealism and Essex's knight-errantry, neither of whom fared very
well in the real theater of European wars. The age of chivalry had
died, the opening scene tells us, with Henry V, and the devastation
in human terms must have been apparent to Londoners in the
late 1580s and early 1590s. Between 1585 and 1602 more than
100,000 men were conscripted to fight abroad and fewer than
half that number returned; in 1591 the largest number in years
were pressed into foreign service – 8,425 – and most of these were
vagabonds, criminals, or volunteers, since militia-men could not be
sent abroad.[6] This levy of men could hardly have gone unnoticed,
and it contrasts strikingly with Essex's chivalric recklessness: his
hawking within enemy territory, his desperate pursuit of fame,
his challenging Villars, the French Catholic commander of Rouen,
to single combat.[7] Moreover, the financial support Elizabeth was
granting Henri IV was sizable – about 60,000 pounds in 1589
alone – and the embattled French king was not paying the English
troops as he promised. This present alliance with Henri, although
he was Protestant and was fighting the Catholic League and the
Spanish for his throne, went against the traditional English enmity
toward France, an enmity the play as a whole depends upon and
stresses. The fundamental difficulty of fighting upon European soil,
whatever the cause, is explicit from the play's beginning and is
crucial later also.

   1 Henry VI does not engage these contemporary concerns directly,
but neither does it ignore them. In an atmosphere of the aspiring Marlovian conqueror, chivalric theatricalism on the part of
Elizabeth's favorite courtiers, and anti-Spanish and anti-Catholic
sentiment in the wake of the Armada's defeat, for a play even
to air the waste and brutality of war, to suggest the evils of

civil dissension, and to begin and conclude with the deaths of warrior-heroes would implicate recent foreign policy and appear subversive to at least the more acute and knowledgeable spectators. Shakespeare's interests in these connections, however, are primarily in how they could be used to dramatize essential conflicts which reoccur on the stage of politics and lead to cultural instability, bad choices and policies, mistakes and disasters, distortions and inversions of value within personal and national realms of action.

If want of men, money, and unity of purpose and strategy abroad, and political factionalism and scheming at home establish the play's thematic concern with disorder, the first scene also reveals a playwright who sees history as problematic, and because it is problematic also theatrical – and contemporary. The variety of contradictory explanation also emphasizes the dramatic potentiality inherent in the process of collective enterprises such as foreign campaigns and a national government collapsing into factional and individual manoeuvrings for power. As the first messenger's realism challenges the absolutes of English courage and honor, the play as a whole undermines the human propensity to romanticize and demonize events and characters, exposing simplifications of the heroic, political, and erotic. The world of *1 Henry VI* becomes darkened by the baseness of motives disclosed, but disorder is not merely the radical inversion of order nor a series of dramatized violations and denials of absolutes, though without a clear teleological movement toward strong closure it might seem so. Its interests lie more in representing the processes of national collapse and the failures of the unifying promises of ideology, and war itself by being staged reveals itself as spectacle. If the theatrical treatment of military conflict is at all inclusive of the pragmatism and truth of war, staged campaigns and skirmishes will necessarily suggest the inhuman elements in the absurdities of battle.

Despite Shakespeare's apparent willingness in the first scene to undermine the simple opposition of English heroism versus French treachery, *1 Henry VI* somewhat uneasily oscillates between the mystifications involved in glorifying the English and demonizing the French and the demystifications of such processes as wishful projections and as partial and actually contributory to the chaos of war. The playwright gives his audience enough popular chauvinism and anti-French sentiment: a Joan of Arc in league with devilish supernatural powers and French aristocrats committed to "policy" and treachery. Joan's demonic athleticism in single combat is twice shown, once to convince Charles of her prowess (I.2) and again to overcome Talbot physically (I.5), and she is shown invoking and pleading with "fiends" (V.3); the unchivalric ambush of Salisbury and Gargrave underscores French treachery (I.4); the Countess of Auvergne tries to capture and execute Talbot (II.3). One might add more to this brief catalog of French antiheroism, but the play clearly demonizes the enemy. At the same time, it undermines the rhetorical excesses that make for such a melodramatic opposition.[8]

If Shakespeare then initiates and promotes the process of demonizing the French by taking over and embellishing the witchcraft and treachery of his chronicle sources, he does so primarily for theatrical reasons. No doubt, a demonic Joan makes for striking effects on the stage and contrasts effectively if unhistorically with the paragon of English courage, Talbot: a scourge of the English against a scourge of the French creates a unifying structural balance in a play otherwise loosely constructed around a miscellany of nobles who at frequent intervals are taken away by death. More to the point perhaps is the dramatic necessity of representing the process of the rhetorical extravagances of displacing the internal problems of the English forces abroad onto the enemy and the process of theatricalizing the war under the unifying banner of Joan, shepherd girl become heroic saint. Lastly, and even more theatrically complex, Joan's witchcraft and the French antiheroism evoke in the spectator a moral superiority which must be foregone once the derision expended upon the enemy is forced upon the English; the play – and in various ways its successors in the tetralogy – produces a strange kind of chauvinistic laughter which later is made to reveal an aspect of grotesque horror.[9]

From the beginning Joan is presented as an impostor. This "holy maid" with visionary powers who will drive "the English forth the bounds of France" (I.2.51–54) amuses the audience in her first appearance by trading courtly love rhetoric with Charles and by mixing amorous dalliance, bawdy innuendo, and double-entendres with her claims to heavenly assistance.[10] Never is there much real tension between Pucelle and Puzzel in the characterization of Joan, and if our moral superiority seems rather too easily extracted throughout the play, the comedy will not be contained within this narrow space. This superiority, augmented by the nationalistic bias the play could depend upon evoking, produces derisive laughter, the kind most often defined by Elizabethan rhetoricians and "psychologists." For example, in his *Arte of Rhetoric* (1553),

Thomas Wilson writes that "the occasion of laughter and the mean that maketh us merry . . . is the foundness, the filthiness, the deformity and all such evil behavior as we see to be in the other . . . ."[11] Even more pertinent is Timothy Bright's explanation in his *Treatise of Melancholie* (1586) for the derivation of "compound perturbations" from "unequal mixtures of liking and misliking": when our joy at having escaped the deformity or evils of others exceeds our "discontent" at their existence, we laugh from a feeling of superiority.[12] The comedy of Joan La Pucelle begins and ends with derisive laughter, but before her final unmasking in the last act the audience's response is complicated by the internalization of the laughter of derision within the play. Sharing in the English lords' mockery of Joan intensifies for the audience the unpleasantness of watching her exulting over her victories, her mocking Bedford and Lucy, and her scoffing over the corpse of Talbot, an unpleasantness which depends upon the initial identification with the English in their derision of Joan. Joan is allowed her moments of military triumph, and the staging most often stresses her superiority; for example, after her successful stratagem of disguising herself and her men as peasants selling corn to get inside the gates of Rouen and retake the city, she and the French lords stand on the walls, as below on the stage the dying Bedford is "brought in sick in a chair":

> *Pucelle*   Good morrow, gallants! Want ye corn for bread?
> I think the duke of Burgundy will fast
> Before he'll buy again at such a rate.
> 'Twas full of darnel; do you like the taste?
>   *Burgundy*   Scoff on, vile fiend and shameless courtezan!
> I trust ere long to choke thee with thy own
> And make thee curse the harvest of that corn.
>   *Dauphin*   Your grace may starve, perhaps, before that time.
>   *Bedford*   O, let no words, but deeds, revenge this treason!
>   *Pucelle*   What will you do, good graybeard? Break a lance,
> And run a tilt at death within a chair?
>   (III.2.41–51)

The theatrical superiority combined with the wry mockery visually and verbally takes away the easy superiority of chauvinistic derision; Joan's deceit may look unheroic but it has worked, and severing military and moral superiority has issued in the triumph of pragmatic, guerilla tactics. Among a number of possible illustrations of this internalization of derision, Joan's response to Lucy's request for the bodies of the Talbots underlines the grotesque humor of the enemy's scorn:

> I think this upstart is old Talbot's ghost,
> He speaks with such a proud commanding spirit.
> For God's sake, let him have them; to keep them here,
> They would but stink and putrefy the air.
>
> (IV.7.87–90)

The sarcasm in its rhetorical surplus balances the melodramatic excesses of the English while consuming whatever chivalric pretense might remain in the romanticism of war, just as Joan has just previously laughed at the "silly stately style" (72) of Lucy's epic catalogue of the slain Talbot's Herculean titles (60–71). Again, visually at the feet of the living French lie the lifeless Talbots, the last remnants of the age of chivalry and the faded glories of Henry V. To be sure, the derisive laughter at Joan's expense returns in the unmasking of her final scene, as the boastful "progeny of kings," miracle worker, and virtuous saint is reduced to revealing her pregnant state to save herself from execution. But all the mockery York and Warwick can muster cannot cancel her military successes or the effectiveness of her sarcastic derision of English folly, baseness, and self-aggrandizement.[13]

The politics of *1 Henry VI* is further complicated by the darkly comic spectacle of factionalism within the English nobility whose fraud, as Lucy says, is more responsible for the death of Talbot and the loss of France than the French forces (IV.4.36–39). The play's third scene reintroduces the bitter feud between Gloucester and Winchester in a way which can only look like farce on the stage. Gloucester's men in blue coats give Winchester's men in tawny coats a beating; the Mayor of London and his officers interrupt, but the scuffling begins again. Most of the derisive insults come from Gloucester (far from the wise counsellor and humanist of *2 Henry VI*), though Winchester is equally acrimonious and haughty. The skirmishes of the men are farcical, and the exchanges of defiance simple, coarse, and bad-natured, counterpointing here and later the sarcastic mockery abroad. The breakdown of order is theatrically, however simply, visualized for the spectator as Crown versus

Church, Gloucester's attempt to examine the munitions in the Tower prevented by Winchester, the administration of the war effort reduced to division and trivialized into reciprocal beard-pulling in "this privileged place" (I.3.44–46). When again the blue and tawny coats "skirmish" and the uncle and great-uncle trade insults and puns, the farce deepens, for even the king himself cannot stop this violent factionalism:

> *K. Henry*   We charge you, on allegiance to ourself,
> To hold your slaughtering hands and keep the peace.
> Pray, uncle Gloucester, mitigate this strife.
> *First Servingman*   Nay, if we be forbidden stones, we'll fall
> to it with our teeth.
> *Second Servingman*   Do what ye dare, we are as resolute.
> *Skirmish again.*
>
> (III.1.86–92)

The "bloody pates" and "resolute" animosity mock any pretense to order even with Henry VI present. After three skirmishes, peace is restored and Gloucester and Winchester reconciled, but each is provided with a one-line aside to underscore the insincerity of the reconciliation and the choric Exeter is furnished with his own insight and ends the scene with a prophesy of "base and envious discord" (187–201).

The Temple Garden scene (II.4), entirely Shakespeare's invention, initiates another set of factions and further trivializes the motives of Henry VI's noblemen. It leads in turn to the vicious squabble between Vernon and Bassett that, along with Falstaff's disgrace, mars Henry's coronation day (IV.1) and to the conflict between York and Somerset over the generalship of the forces in France. Other incidents of pettiness and division among the English lords could further amplify this factionalism; clearly the internal problems will not be displaced by demonizing the French. The wilfulness of the English aristocrats arrogantly overrules the law in the midst of the Inns of Court; the "argument" is kept in the "scabbard"; the truth may be determined by plucking roses and throwing down gages. The English demonize each other, and the veneer of courteous formality only makes the venality beneath shine the brighter.

To some modern readers this extensive emphasis upon factional conflict suggests the playwright's endorsement of the Tudor myth of a longer historical cycle begun with the curse of Bolingbroke's usurpation and redeemed by Henry VII; to others Shakespeare here begins his theatrical brooding about the evils of disunity and the consequences of civil dissension.[14] Although these elements are present in *1 Henry VI*, they are not prominent, and the play seems very little like a lesson in order taught through its negations. If Shakespeare uses his historical hindsight to provide Warwick and Exeter with prophecies of disasters to come, Warwick grossly underestimates the casualties at a thousand (II.4.127) and Exeter himself says that he sees no more than what is "so plain" (III.1.200) that any "simple man" can "see" it (IV.1.187): loss of France and continued discord among the nobility. The unhistorical capture of Joan by Plantagenet, now Duke of York, is determined more by the structural demands of this play than by the next, and nothing really deflects our gaze beyond these spectacles of chaos. The second view would imply a serious concern for the possibilities of civil discontent and rebellion and establish a conservative playwright preaching the doctrine of the Homilies. To some extent this appears a well-founded interpretation, given the topicality I discussed earlier in this section; whatever the judgments of modern historians, many Elizabethans did point to factionalism in Court and Council and saw it at least partly as arising from the wars in the Low Countries and in France, and if Shakespeare is warning against the evils of disunity, who else could he be addressing but the nobles? But to read *1 Henry VI* primarily in either of these ways will distort the play.

In what is probably the earliest of his plays, Shakespeare seems more intent upon mapping out the political landscape and upon clearing the territory of the historical explanations which obscure the workings of history.[15] The repeated interruptions, violations, and other underminings of formality – from the first scene on – bring into question the monumental, the ceremonial, and the static conception of history and politics which the chronicles and the popular imagination assume and which those who appear to have made and to make history act upon. The basic intention might be summarized as deflation through comedy and irony, deflation of certainty and authority, heroism and patriotism. The Temple Garden scene imagines for the spectator how the War of the Roses might have originated; really quite unnecessary in the play and formally detachable from it, it shows us witty but shallow noblemen turning an historic moment into aetheticized form, stripping law and right of their objective existence, counting roses – in a theater named The Rose – in order to decide upon the truth. History is not as innocent as we would like it to be and its actors far more childish than we would want them to be; in the Temple Garden scene, the characters are highly conscious of their actions and language – formal, conceited, punning, wittily insulting – yet totally unconscious of their absurdity. On the other hand, Joan, for example, can set up a scene as a performance and demonstrate her clever manipulation of the political arts of rhetoric: she tells Charles, the Bastard of Orleans, and Alencon that she will "entice the Duke of Burgundy To leave the Talbot and follow us" by using "fair persuasions, mix'd with sugar'd words" (III.3.18–20); Burgundy then enters and becomes completely "bewitch'd" with "her words" (58); Joan comments "Done like a Frenchman! [*Aside.*] – turn and turn again" (85). We have seen a performance, bracketed by an announcement and closed by stressing sarcastically its success.

FROM CEREMONY TO "PRACTICE"

Perhaps the most remarkable character who attempts to perform according to his role is King Henry VI, whose performances are repeatedly interrupted by the fluctations of human passions and the unpredictability of history. He does not appear until the third act, and then he ineffectively tries to quell the hostility between his uncles:

> Uncles of Gloucester and of Winchester,
> The special watchmen of our English weal,
> I would prevail, if prayers might prevail,
> To join your hearts in love and amity.
> O, what a scandal is it to our crown
> That two such noble peers as ye should jar!
> Believe me, lords, my tender years can tell
> Civil dissension is a viperous worm
> That gnaws the bowels of the commonwealth.
> (III.1.65–73)

Ideologically, this exactly correct appeal to national unity under the supreme "crown" of the monarch belatedly instructs the realm's protectors in their duties, but the discord has grown too cancerous, having filtered down to the servants of these lords who have resorted to stones after the Mayor of London has forbidden them to carry arms of any kind. Henry VI has no power to stop the rock throwing or even to silence the animosity. The scene is sadly comic as the king is shouted down by common servants and reduced to tears. He pleads to his uncle, the bishop, to end the "discord" that "doth afflict" his "soul":

> Can you, my Lord of Winchester, behold
> My sighs and tears, and will not once relent?
> Who should be pitiful, if it be not you?
> Or who shall study to prefer a peace
> If holy churchmen take delight in broils?
> (107–11)

What Henry says seems "right" enough, but it is mixed with special pleading based upon an appeal to his own person and not to his monarchical prerogative of ruling his subjects. Also apparently wise, he reconciles his uncles and then hears the petition Warwick urges on behalf of Richard Plantagenet. In forcing the "friendship" of Gloucester and Winchester, he has ended these skirmishes, acted benevolently, and managed to send the servants off to the surgeon and tavern; in restoring the titles and inheritance of Plantagenet, he would seem to be co-opting a potent adversary, righting an injustice, and gaining a powerful nobleman's loyalty. He even appears to play the role effectively by accepting Plantagenet's vows of true service and performing with propriety the ritual of the subject's kneeling and the monarch's re-naming: the king incorporates the energy of his possible enemies by appropriating it.

On stage, the "bloody pates" are replaced by a decisive action on Henry's part: he seems to be growing into the role before our eyes as his performance becomes more regal and effective. The choric Exeter, however, underlines the "plain" falsity of the appearances. Several scenes later the young king again plays out his role according to its prescribed formalities: Talbot, momentarily triumphant, kneels at the palace in Paris before Henry, who praises him fulsomely and creates him Earl of Shrewsbury (III.4.26). The theatrical pairing of the formally similar kneelings and namings highlights for the audience the hollowness of regal ceremony: the false subject Plantagenet/York and the true servant Talbot participate in formally identical moments in the display of authority. Clearly, the ceremonial and symbolic are not sufficient even when they are not interrupted or flouted.[16]

Act IV begins with Henry's coronation in Paris, followed immediately by another kneeling before the king, this time by the Governor of Paris, who is administered an oath of allegiance by Gloucester. This ceremony too is quickly revealed as empty, as the cowardly Falstaff enters, is stripped of his "Garter" and knighthood by the heroic Talbot and sent "packing" by the king. News that the Duke of Burgundy has revolted causes the king to send Talbot after him, and Vernon and Basset enter to crave combat over the proper color of roses to wear as badges. Henry attempts to resolve this dispute by putting on a red rose and by making York and Somerset share the generalship of the English forces in France. The "solution" provides another false reconciliation and aggravates the divisions among the noblemen. Warwick sarcastically remarks that Henry "Prettily, methought, did play the orator" (IV.1.175), York rankles, and Exeter ends the scene with another choric soliloquy prophesying "More rancorous spite, more furious raging broils" (185).

Henry does indeed rise to the oratorical occasion; he says the "right" things:

> Henceforth I charge you, as you love our favour,
> Quite to forget this quarrel, and the cause.
> And you, my lords, remember where we are:
> In France, amongst a fickle wavering nation;
> If they perceive dissension in our looks,
> And that within ourselves we disagree,
> How will their grudging stomachs be provok'd
> To wilful disobedience, and rebel!
> Beside, what infamy will there arise
> When foreign princes shall be certified
> That for a toy, a thing of no regard,
> King Henry's peers and chief nobility
> Destroy'd themselves, and lost the realm of France!
> O, think upon the conquest of my father,
> My tender years, and let us not forgo
> That for a trifle that was bought with blood!
> Let me be umpire in this doubtful strife.
> I see no reason if I wear this rose, [*putting on a red rose*]

That any one should therefore be suspicious
I incline more to Somerset than York:
Both are my kinsmen, and I love them both . . .
                        (135-55)

The roses are things "of no regard," of no intrinsic meaning, and
the king's rhetoric here impeccably dissects the consequences of
discord. Those who would see Henry VI merely as a weak and
boyish ruler must contend with the high heroics of this and other
speeches; they have the proper regal authority, even though the
king's decisiveness works against him.

Describing the Royal Shakespeare Company's 1977-78 production of the play, David Daniell singles out the ironies of Henry's
performance of his kingly role:

> The complex knot of dramatic forces at the coronation, with
> the news of Burgundy and the York-Somerset quarrel, makes
> a firmly Shakespearian scene. The child king punctures Duke
> Humphrey of Gloucester's wrath with the line "What! doth my
> uncle Burgundy revolt?" This Henry, though young, finds his
> own authority rapidly. From nervously appealing to Gloucester
> over his shoulder when faced with Talbot, to gently making the
> thirty-line sermon to the two factions, Alan Howard allowed him
> to grow in both force and innocence at once. The King is the
> focus of the scene, and the clash of his worst possible solutions
> with his highest possible intentions makes the sort of ironic
> resonant effect we usually associate with later Shakespeare.
> Henry makes three great mistakes, sending his one devotedly
> loyal and disinterested follower, Talbot, away: choosing one rose,
> the red one, and - played here as an afterthought - splitting the
> command in France. Howard suggests that there might be ironies
> in Henry here: more, there might be something closer to home,
> something at the root like sheer humanity, the ordinary capacity
> to make crashing mistakes and not see. Howard's Henry in his
> new self-confidence in France suddenly sees himself as a Good
> King, in the delight of growing up, not because of any unique
> royal circumstances.[17]

What Henry does not see is that common sense - everything he says
is, after all, true - and the heroic call to unity will not work. The
three kneelings demonstrate Henry's naive belief in the capacity

of ritual to order the world, the "sermon" against dissension the capacity of rhetoric, and the "three mistakes" the capacity of well-meant decisiveness. The staging and the language mock this faith in the adequate performance of the king's role; without a strong Henry the irony is severely lessened, for one of his functions in the play's re-creation of history is to underscore the insufficiency of a static conception of monarchical ritual, rhetoric, and narrowly defined role prescription. The "Good King" belongs to the morality plays and political interludes; on the stage of historical politics it is unfortunately out of place, often almost comic in its innocence. At the beginning of Act V, Henry openly appears relieved that negotiation will replace war:

> Ay, marry, uncle, for I always thought
> It was both impious and unnatural
> That such immanity and bloody strife
> Should reign among professors of one faith.
> (V.1.11–14)

The inappropriateness of the Christian king seems decidedly comic, even if his pacific sentiments are in another sense worthy of praise.

The world of *1 Henry VI* is an inverted world, and Henry acts as if it were not. History is not ordered by restoring dukedoms, creating earldoms, administering oaths of allegiance – and, finally, not by trading provinces for marriageable daughters of titular kings. As with Joan La Pucelle, the audience is left feeling uncomfortably superior to the naive Henry, whose cumulative imperceptiveness evokes various ironies ranging from the comic to the darkly sardonic. The backstairs of politics occupies the stage of politics at the end of the play, as Suffolk manipulates both Henry and Margaret; in fact, these last few scenes might be subtitled "capturing the stage" with Suffolk in soliloquy having gained center-stage:

> Margaret shall now be Queen, and rule the King;
> But I will rule her, the King, and realm.
> (V.5.107–8)

Henry VI has wilfully submitted to the marriage with Reignier's daughter against his better political and personal judgment, foregoing the Good King role in the hopes of ending the war and going to bed with the ravishing Margaret, and in the bargain taxing "the

people . . . a tenth" to fetch her and her worthless titles (93).[18] In this anarchic world, only Talbot is really exempt from feminine dominance. Joan uses sex to gain power, and Margaret captivates Suffolk, who momentarily resists betraying his better instincts as a loyal husband. Even the Bishop of Winchester is accused of being "froward by nature . . . Lascivious, wanton" (III.1.18–19). The dominance of women and of the iconographical concupiscence (frowardness) of the feminine complements the other comic patterns in the play; indeed, this was one way that Sidney defined "comedy" in his *Defense of Poesy*:

> So in *Hercules*, painted with his great beard, and furious countenance, in a womans attyre, spinning, at *Omphales* commaundement, it breedes both delight and laughter: for the representing of so straunge a power in Love, procureth delight, and the scornfulnesse of the action, stirreth laughter.[19]

Shakespeare's inversions are not so farcical as this, but the principles are similar, as the Venus and Mars and Helen and Paris allusions suggest. Once again, the laughter of derision, of scorn, helps us to define the dark comedy of *1 Henry VI* and the unpleasantly superior attitude of the spectator. The undeniably traditional comic gambits of unmasking – stripping the cowardly Falstaff's garter, exposing Joan's imitation of the Virgin Mary – and of the trickster tricked – the Countess of Auvergne and Joan – evoke varying degrees of superiority and derision. Yet in the end the audience is left feeling sympathetic to no one but the dead Talbots. Henry's unintentional mistakes in setting up his enemy the Duke of York and in plucking the red rose actively involve him in the play's muddle of errors as does the sequence of false reconciliations, but the marriage to Margaret and the unconscionable tax on the people make us question his sincerity in playing the Good King as well as make us smile at his naivete in choosing that role. Desiring "fruition of her love" (V.5.9), Henry follows his will rather than acts his regal role, again disclosing the ceremonial as a mask worn on state occasions, and as Suffolk's allusion implies Margaret will be a Helen to England, bringing confusion and war to her captors (104–6).

   Henry V, Bedford, Salisbury, and the Talbots have been replaced by Winchester, York, and Suffolk, the chivalric by the cunning and manipulative, the ceremonial by the Machiavellian and sexual, English honor by French fraud. By projecting the "practice" of such self-aggrandizing craft into the 1400s, Shakespeare essentially collapses the decentralization of warring feudal lords and the Machiavellianism of contemporary political thinking and thereby demonstrates that the "new politics" is simply the old anarchy of the Wars of the Roses rewritten. If this seems a conservative stance, he too clearly undermines the ceremonial rituals of monarchy, revealing them as belonging to an archaic world of chivalry in which the devoted Talbot, kneeling loyally before his king, dying bravely with his son, provides an emblematic and static image of an age long past.

At least this was the way Thomas Nashe described the play in *Piers Pennilesse* (1592). The implicit explanation for its success in Nashe's account lies in the play's moving combination of tragedy, English history, and heroic drama, a combination not unique but rather representative of a prevailing tradition within the then current genres of the professional theater and one whose didactic lessons about the courage of the past could be used to reprove "these degenerate effeminate dayes of ours" and so to defend the stage against its detractors. Nashe, however, also rightly captures the power of theatrical illusion in describing the magical reappearance of Talbot, who though dead for two hundred years now triumphs "againe on the Stage" and evokes the tears of the audience "who, in the Tragedian who represents his person, imagine they behold him fresh bleeding."[20] Most of the first audiences came for this re-presentational magic, few for the "reproofe" of the present, for the lessons in providence Nashe saw in the play, for a demonstration of the Tudor myth, or for the initial installment of an eight-part series with Respublica as the hero, yet *1 Henry VI* cannot accurately be described as the "tragedy of Talbot" nor does it fulfil the expectations we might suppose the Elizabethan spectator might have brought to the theater in 1590 or 1592. Shakespeare seems quite intent upon keeping Talbot human as well as heroic and appears to have deliberately avoided the Marlovian propensity for mythic proportions and given most of the gaudy rhetoric of the Marlovian conqueror to the French, especially to the Dauphin. Nor is it easy to see *1 Henry VI* as inspiring much patriotic feeling among its spectators or to find in it the light comedy and farce of many of the non-Marlovian "historical" plays which precede it or to discover the "morality of state" which was central to other contemporary plays. Shakespeare's play opposes the Marlovian conception of history, severely circumscribes the official Tudor myth of history, eschews the popular Armada rhetoric, ignores political allegories of good and bad government, and presents its comic dimensions in ways which may be as savage and cruel as Marlowe's but which point toward a sophisticated interdependence of barbarism and civilization. Even in a play as early as 1 *Henry VI*, the key to Shakespeare's dramatic art (and also his distinctiveness as a playwright) lies in understanding his sense of the theater and the theatrical in politics.

3

Henry VI, Part Two

MADNESS AND BUTCHERY

In *2 Henry VI* the violence escalates into madness and butchery. Although the ironies turn sardonic and prophetic in the last act of Part 1, the memory of the brave Talbots and the comic relish of Joan's exposure and condemnation provide enough heroism and laughter to keep the darkness of history from completely engulfing that play. Part 2 in contrast becomes considerably more savage, as Shakespeare fills the unfolding tragedy of Henry's reign with deaths more gruesome, conspiracies more vicious, parodies of chivalry more grotesque and farcical, lords more ruthlessly ambitious, and politics more unredeemable. Except perhaps for the increasingly ineffectual king, pushed even further towards the margins of history, none of the characters is capable of enlisting the audience's sympathy for more than a moment; seldom do we become more than spectators of this horror show of bloody self-seeking among the predators in this jungle beyond the machiavellian landscape of Part 1. Humphrey Duke of Gloucester wishes to see himself as the loyal counsellor to the king, dispensing justice in an impartial manner, yet his "humanist" judgments are undercut by the triviality of the cases, and his continuing battle with great-uncle Beaufort, the Bishop of Winchester now Cardinal, also undermines his credibility.[1] Alexander Iden, loyal squire and conqueror of Jack Cade, and Lord Say, another humanist jurist, are totally representative figures, performing their brave resistance to anarchy briefly before they disappear from the plot. The play ends with York and his three sons – and the "law" of the scabbard for which they stand – in the ascendancy.

The stage itself reinforces the ugliness of this naked power's gaining control. When alarums and excursions, battles and skirmishes, are staged, the theater tends to diminish the grandeur and romanticism of war; in Part 1 the guerrilla tactics of the French perfectly fit the scale of the stage: ambush and disguise play more realistically than chivalry. As the action is moved indoors to the court, rather than having a diminutive effect, the stage magnifies violence: the murder of Gloucester in his own bed becomes more shocking by virtue of its singularity and its aberration from the normal business of making policy and even of pursuing political intrigues. Similarly, moved from the fields of France to the streets of London, violence on stage calls attention to its disruption of the everyday life of commerce and relative safety. Part 2 saves the battlefield for Act V, but by then the Battle of St. Alban's seems a rather tame, albeit logical, outcome of the furious politics which has preceded it.

Another addition to the political landscape of Part 2 is the commons, an element absent from Part 1. Again, the stage itself by its very nature provides an essentially subversive subplot whenever those of lower status than kings and noblemen become part of the theatrical action. Ideologically, the most often invisible populace has become sufficiently worthy of attention to be represented at all as part of English history. Theatrically, as soon as ordinary soldiers, citizens, and peasants are brought upon the stage, the asymmetry of rank, class, wealth, costume, and manners becomes immediately apparent, and these disparities become dramatic contrasts. Much of the time, the contrasts result in comedy – a topic more fully discussed in the next section – but comedy seldom can be confined to a laughter of derision at the aristocracy's inferiors in riches and literacy; however conservative, it exposes the arbitrary element in the dependence upon and deference to authority. The lower classes by their very presence expand the definition of society to include more than the elites of its top layer; more of the whole nation must be accounted for politically and economically: the arena of ideological contest is broadened. In *2 Henry VI* York "uses" Jack Cade for his own political purposes, clearly exposing the exploitative nature of the aristocratic machiavellianism whose moorings are closer to the 1590s than to the 1450s; Cade as York's pawn was solely Shakespeare's addition to his chronicle sources. Although Cade's rebellion is an extreme case of what happens when the commons join the dramatis personae, some opposition of values as well as some sense of the asymmety of resources seems inevitable by the very nature of the theater: the battle for the right to occupy the stage mirrors naturally the struggles for power in the larger social world beyond the auditorium.

Several other considerations force themselves upon the audience in *2 Henry VI*. The marginal classes are not merely acknowledged by the theater; they threaten the boundaries between the aristocracy and the usually invisible artisans and peasants and eventually attempt to displace them. Second, they undermine the generic unity which Nashe saw in Part 1 by radically challenging the coherence of epic, history, and dramatic tragedy. Joan's peasant origins, vulgarity, and fiendish associations do not drastically alter Part 1's insistence upon the element of tragedy, because it confines its cast to royal family, a few prominent nobles and clergy, and the equally aristocratic opponents of the English, but Part 2 by introducing theatrically unfamiliar characters turns any such generic expectations into chaos, revealing in the process the historical grounding of such unity, however tenuous, in aesthetic, social, and ideological exclusiveness as well as its incompleteness as an interpretive approach to English history. Third, in representing the socially marginal on stage, drama encounters a problem with which narrative can deal with more detachment, especially if the fiction wishes to demonize and depose of the rebellious with dispatch. Sidney's chivalric princes and Spenser's Artegall and Talus violently eliminate lower class rebels as just so much criminal nuisance, reasserting the superiority of the noble by dispensing with the banditry threatening the commonwealth. On stage the physical impersonation of character makes it difficult to represent rebellious peasants as nameless, faceless, mechanical, and dehumanized. Shakespeare's rebels are named and placed: "Jack Cade the clothier" from Kent, "Best's son, the tanner of Wingham," "Dick the Butcher," "Smith the Weaver" (IV.2.4,21,25,28). If the last three are unhistorical, the mere naming nevertheless touches them with some small humanity to complement their theatrical reality; whatever they might do, they can not be so easily dismissed as could the villainous of narrative romance.[2]

Continuing the direction of Part 1, 2 *Henry VI* presents us with the world beyond chivalry. Apart from some limited courtly posturing, the rhetoric of honor and heroism on the field of battle has been replaced by conspiracy and intrigue, trumped up charges and murder; the heroic self-assertion that could at times be military and nationalistic (if at times often hollow) in Part 1 has become more Marlovian and Machiavellian. In Part 1 Salisbury is ambushed, Talbot is almost trapped by the Countess of Auvergne, and finally the Talbots are cornered; the guerrilla tactics of the French illustrate new possibilities in the guiles of war. Part 2 not only takes such guilefulness away from the military arena which might in some way justify it, but also makes the plots that are laid the open subject of unabashed discussion. The play self-reflexively comments upon its own plotting, as the schemes of destruction are either foreshadowed or announced, then acted out; the audience is told of the traps, then shown the victims ensnared. Suffolk assures Queen Margaret that she need not fear Eleanor, Gloucester's wife:

> Madam, myself have lim'd a bush for her,
> And plac'd a quire of such enticing birds
> That she will light to listen to their lays,
> And never mount to trouble you again.
> (I.3.88–91)

In the next scene we are shown the apprehension of her co-conspirators in necromancy, an arrest which spells her downfall in the next act. York, who has helped engineer this snare and who captures them, comments:

> Lord Buckingham, methinks you watch'd her well:
> A pretty plot, well chosen to build upon!
> (I.4.54–55)

The political and theatrical merge, as surveillant and spectator become identified through the pun. Later, when Eleanor in disgrace, "barefoot in a white sheet," meets her husband in the streets, she picks up the image of "liming" to warn him that Suffolk

> And York, and impious Beaufort, that false priest,
> Have all lim'd bushes to betray thy wings;
> And, fly thou how thou canst, they'll tangle thee:
> But fear not thou, until thou foot be snar'd,
> Nor never seek prevention of thy foes.
> (II.4.53–57)[3]

In the next scene, these three accuse Gloucester before the king, and seeing his denials are futile, Gloucester describes the proceedings as a morality interlude run amok:

> Ah! gracious lord, these days are dangerous.

> Virtue is chok'd with foul Ambition,
> And Charity chas'd hence by Rancour's hand;
> Foul Subornation is predominant,
> And Equity exil'd your Highness' land.
> I know their complot is to have my life . . . .
>   (III.1.142–47)[4]

In this plotting, his own death

>   is made the prologue to their play;
> For thousands more, that yet suspect no peril,
> Will not conclude their plotted tragedy.
>   (150–52)

After this defense and the exit of Henry VI, who is convinced of Gloucester's innocence, Queen Margaret, Suffolk, York, and the Cardinal evince an even stronger determination to destroy the Lord Protector; Suffolk puts it as bluntly as possible:

> And do not stand on quillets how to slay him:
> Be it by gins, by snares, by subtlety,
> Sleeping or waking, 'tis no matter how,
> So he be dead; for that is good deceit
> Which mates him first that first intends deceit.
>   (261–65)

The next scene begins with a short exchange between Duke Humphrey's two hired murderers and proceeds to bring his dead body upon the stage, thus completing "prologue" and "complot."

These scenes and others like them dramatize a world beyond ceremony as well as beyond chivalry. Private scenes of secret plotting alternate with public scenes in which insults and threats are traded or plots are accomplished through vigorous accusation and perverted trial or through the violence of the conspirators'greater numbers.[5] Repeatedly the audience sees groups against an individual, a pair of characters, or a smaller group: Gloucester, Salisbury, Warwick, and York against Henry and Suffolk over the marriage and Suffolk's being made duke; York, Buckingham, and their guard against Margery Jourdain and Bolingbroke; Suffolk, the Cardinal, York, and the Queen against Gloucester; Warwick, Salisbury, and "many commons" against Suffolk; the Lieutenant, Walter Whitmore, and soldiers against the imprisoned Suffolk; Cade and his rebels against the Clerk of Chartham, Matthew Goffe, and Lord Say; York and his Irish army against the King and Somerset; York and his sons triumphant in the last scene. Among these, the "crowd" scenes, however they might be staged, provide enough non-speaking extras – guard, commons, soldiers, rebels, and Irish army – to dramatize emphatically a world in which naked force has triumphed. Violent men under the command of determined, singleminded leaders at regular intervals capture the stage of politics, and other assorted minor characters – the murderers, the Cliffords – add to the madness pervading the action and rhetoric of 2 *Henry VI* and directing the brutality which ironically overshadows the talk of subtle snares and the craft of liming trees for unsuspecting birds. This is the world of butchery, of dark fantasy and nightmare.⁶

But whose nightmare? Surely, the readiest answer is that the nightmare originates with the playwright who structured and added to the chroniclers' history and becomes the experience of the audiences who respond to it. Beyond the stage itself, such considerations are crucial, and I will later return to them. Within the play, the nightmare belongs mostly to Henry VI and Margaret.⁷ Although 2 *Henry VI* begins with the King in control, before the opening scene proceeds far, the unsatisfactory financial terms of his marriage of Margaret of Reignier have alienated his entire court, including his uncle and the Lord Protector, who cannot hide his shock at the absolute stupidity of the arrangement to deliver Anjou and Maine to the bride's father, and who proceeds to "unload his grief" (I.1.75) to the other nobles after the departure of Henry, Margaret, and Suffolk. Henry quickly becomes a marginal character, partly from weakness, partly from choice; he takes on the dramatic function more simply performed by Exeter in Part 1: the function of directing the audience's response to the unfolding events. Exeter, however, provides choric commentary apart from the scenes themselves; Henry is involved in and somehow also detached from events, serving as a much more complex indicator of possible responses to the mounting evils of anarchy. Henry is almost alone in believing in the providential nature of history, and the rhythms of shock at the darkness of human nature and assurance of the rightness of God's plan in these apparently unjust proceedings form a minor pattern in the play. The discovery of the evil and demonic face of his subjects creates Henry's nightmare, and his realization of his powerlessness to act in any way to redirect events extends that nightmare. His religion makes ruling well both important and impossible and further deepens the horrors he perceives. However ineffective he may be, Henry's perspective provides an indirect commentary upon the pervasive madness and influences our responses to it.

Queen Margaret's nightmare begins almost immediately after the marriage but takes a different form. Expecting her husband to be another Suffolk, a handsome courtier and powerful monarch, she is sorely disappointed; she tells Suffolk:

> I thought King Henry had resembled thee
> In courage, courtship, and proportion:
> But all his mind is bent to holiness,
> To number Ave-Maries on his beads;
> His champions are the prophets and apostles,
> His weapons holy saws of sacred writ,
> His study is his tilt-yard, and his loves
> Are brazen images of canoniz'd saints.
> I would the college of the Cardinals
> Would choose him Pope, and carry him to Rome,
> And set the triple crown upon his head:
> That were a state fit for his Holiness.
>   (I.3.53–64)

She laments that the "least" of Henry's nobles "can do more in England than the King" (70–71). With the hindsight of the two last plays of the first tetralogy, Margaret has often been seen as the French tigress or as the screech-owl who will do anything to maintain her power, but in *2 Henry VI* that toughness has not reached its maturity. This speech evidences her disappointment with Henry but not her unwillingness to see this marriage through. Her very long speech later (III.1.72–120) explains her own nightmare to her husband, who, it would seem, hardly listens and who does not respond. Henry, like Aeneas, has abandoned her, and she, like Dido, consoles herself with Suffolk, her Ascanius. England has not turned out to be Troynovant, and she has left her home and family and suffered a frightening sea passage for a man who will not share anything with her and who barely acknowledges her; she is "more wretched than" the murdered Gloucester, whose death distracts her husband. If the adulterous triangle ends in Suffolk's beheading and Margaret's grief, the excess of her embracing her lover's severed head does not cancel her sentiments for her husband. When the two had parted (III.2), Margaret could not have known Suffolk would come to this cruel, grotesque end. Though Henry upbraids her for this grief, her reply stresses her love for her husband:

> *King* How, madam! Still lamenting Suffolk's death?
> I fear me, love, if that I had been dead,
> Thou wouldest not have mourn'd so much for me.
> *Queen* My love; I should not mourn, but die for thee.
>   (IV.4.21–24)[8]

This Margaret is anything but shrill, and in the next scene in which she appears, she is completely silent, as Henry makes decisions about how to handle York and Cade and gives orders (that are obeyed) to Somerset and Buckingham. The scene ends with the King's resolution, tinged with sadness and ambivalence:

> Come, wife, let's in, and learn to govern better;
> For yet may England curse my wretched reign.
>   (IV.9.47–48)

At the Battle of St. Albans she becomes more vocal and active, but her determination results partly from the necessity to counter Henry's fatalistic inertia and issues in the decision to regroup their forces in London, where they can re-establish themselves with the support of their loyal subjects (V.2.77–83). If this would mean her survival as well, this last image in the play of the royal couple adds to its binding their nightmares together.

Henry and Margaret arrive at the margins of history by different paths. Margaret had expected "courage, courtship, and proportion" from Henry, a courtly world of chivalry and ceremony in which the monarch would rule and her "champions" defend her against all comers, but Henry shies away from the exercise of power and both her "champions" – Suffolk and Somerset – are killed. Henry's nightmare, to a large extent, originates in his misconception of his kingly role. He sees himself as a peace-maker, and making peace most often for him means avoiding strife: he is reluctant to create conflict by deciding between York and Somerset for Regent of

France (I.3.102); he tries to mediate the animosity between Margaret and Eleanor (143), between Suffolk and Gloucester (II.1.32–34) and the Cardinal and Gloucester (56–59); he finally succumbs to the nobles' persecution of Gloucester to end their feuding (III.1.195–96); he will send "some holy bishop" to "entreat" or himself go to "parley" with Cade to end his rebellion (IV.4.8–13); he sends Buckingham to meet York but advises his emissary to "be not too rough in terms" with the traitor, who is fierce and "cannot brook hard language" (V.1.83–84). His intentions are impeccable, inappropriate, and ineffectual: he attempts to calm the fury of malicious insults by advising his court that "blessed are the peacemakers on earth," only to be answered by his great-uncle, the Cardinal:

> Let me be blessed for the peace I make
> Against this proud Protector with my sword!
> (II.1.32–34)

He would "poise" Gloucester's "cause in Justice' equal scales, Whose beam stands sure, whose rightful cause prevails" (196–97), but events mock his intentions.

Henry's powerlessness to prevent strife and ensure justice is for him a nightmare challenging his self-conception and his faith in God's providence; he simply cannot understand the "darkness" which has engulfed Gloucester:

> What low'ring star now envies thy estate,
> That these great lords, and Margaret our Queen,
> Do seek subversion of thy harmless life?
> Thou never didst them wrong, nor no man wrong.
> (III.1.206–9)

His remedy is to grieve, to weep and withdraw, to faint at the news of Gloucester's death and then to wish for his own death (III.2.s.d.32, 53–54). In the next scene, faced with the Cardinal's dying unrepentant and in agony, Henry responds to his great-uncle's horrible confession of guilt in murdering Gloucester by calling upon God to look upon him with mercy. He pleads with the Cardinal to think on "heaven's bliss" but to no avail:

> *King* He dies, and makes no sign. O God, forgive him!

Warwick So bad a death argues a monstrous life.
King Forbear to judge, for we are sinners all.
Close up his eyes, and draw the curtain close;
And let us all to meditation.

(III.3.29–33)

Henry once again is characteristically protecting his religious faith
from the shocks of evil, just as he had asked forgiveness from
God for suspecting foul play in Gloucester's death (III.2.135–39).
That faith suffers much and desperately looks for confirmation:
ironically in the Simpcox "miracle" (II.1.66–67), in the "justice" of
the farcical trial by combat between Horner and Peter (II.3.97–101),
in the unexpected dispersal of Cade's rebels (IV.9.13–14). He is even
willing to excuse Cade's rebels:

O graceless men! they know not what they do.

(IV.4.37)

and York's treason:

Ay, Clifford; a bedlam and ambitious humour
Makes him oppose himself against his king.

(V.1.132–33)

His religious faith at first leads him to hope – "Come, Margaret;
God, our hope, will succour us" (IV.4.54) – but later to political
fatalism – "Can we outrun the heavens? Good Margaret, stay"
(V.2.73), an acceptance of God's judgment of his failure to reign
and his last words in Part 2. That such a reluctance to judge
and such a naive faith are inappropriate in a monarch in the
end seems beside the point; they provide vantage points from
which to measure the madness and atrocity around the king,
scripturally based positions tenaciously held which conflict with
the realities of violence he must face. Ironically, Henry, so fond
of quoting from the Psalms and Gospels, is finally left with only
his queen and one defender, the Young Clifford, bitter over his
father's death, his violent nature as raw, malicious, and pitiless
as York's. Through the characterization of the king, Shakespeare
engages and distances his audience: he has illuminated the darkness

of history through Henry's nightmarish education in its horrors yet at the same time so painted the political folly of his king's values that we accept the rightness of his defeat, the justice of York's dismissal:

> No, thou art not king;
> Not fit to govern and rule multitudes,
> Which dar'st not, no, nor canst not rule a traitor.
> That head of thine doth not become a crown.
> (V.1.93–96)

There could be no stronger contrast of values between Henry's self-conception as the Christian peace-maker and York's Achillean heroism:

> That gold must round engirt these brows of mine,
> Whose smile and frown, like to Achilles' spear,
> Is able with the change to kill and cure.
> (99–101)

Nightmare though it may be, there can be no doubt of the authority that York's claim does and will command.[9]

SAVAGE COMEDY AND THE AUDIENCE'S NIGHTMARE

Whose nightmare? The common citizens of England recurrently invade the stage of politics in *2 Henry VI* and often turn the proceedings into farce. As in Part 1, the ceremonial world of royalty and nobility is violated by interruption, but the comic scenes in Part 2 do much more than undermine the pretensions of political formality and ordered ritual. Though the laughter occasioned by illiterate and foolish commoners does frequently lighten the darkness of this mad world of anarchy, its primary function is ultimately to darken it further, to intensify and broaden the nightmare of history, until the anarchy threatens to spill over into the audience.[10] The inclusion of so much more of the social world extends this dark fantasy into almost every corner, and the laughter evoked turns ambivalent, cruel, sardonic, and grotesque on most occasions. If the influence of Marlowe is apparent in much of the first tetralogy's comic scenes, Shakespeare's grotesque is far more complicated than the Marlovian *Schadenfreude*, his derisive and cruel laughter at the unfortunate.[11] Marlowe seldom presents us with victims with positive virtues and human faces and, except for *Edward II*, a play probably written after *2 Henry VI*, sets his savage mockery in a locale distinct from England and less immediate in its historical basis; the victims of the Guise and the virgins of Damascus are only sketches, but the bodies which lie scattered on Shakespeare's stage belong to English lords and citizens, and in Part 2 (and later plays in the tetralogy) this dance-of-death is exclusively an Englsh affair. The scenes of humorous farce turning perversely cruel are elaborated in a more complex and careful way than Marlowe's: they are deliberately calculated to force upon the audience something very near what Eliot called Marlowe's "savage comic humor," but they also take away some of the defense mechanisms against horror and atrocity which lessen the impact of Marlowe's ugly comedy.[12]

Each of the three obviously comic sequences – Peter and Horner, the Simpcoxes, and Cade's rebellion – begins in innocent enough high spirits and in laughter which seems safe enough, but only the briefest of these – the Saunder Simpcox scene – does not turn bloody and it has its own ambivalent resonances. Each also underscores the social discontent among the people, the various exploitative measures of the powerful classes, and the difficulties of keeping the poor and powerless off the stage of politics. In addition to these sequences, a number of other incidents and references emphasize that the preferred theaters for aristocratic display – foreign battlefield and courtly tournament – are absent from this anarchic world beyond chivalry and ceremony.

In the commons' first appearance, their dissatisfaction with their lot is controlled and polite: three or four petitioners waylay the Queen and Suffolk and deliver their "supplications in the quill," mistaking Suffolk for the Lord Protector. The brief business of these petitions opens the ambivalent pattern of comedy and discontent in the play:

> 1 *Petitioner* Mine is, and't please your Grace, against John Goodman, my Lord Cardinal's man, for keeping my house, and lands, and wife, and all, from me.
> *Suffolk* Thy wife too! that's some wrong indeed. What's yours? What's here! [*Reads.*] "Against the Duke of Suffolk,

for enclosing the commons of Long Melford." How now,
sir knave!

2 Pet. Alas! sir, I am but a poor petitioner of our whole
township.

Peter Against my master, Thomas Horner, for saying that
the Duke of York was rightful heir to the crown.

Queen What say'st thou? Did the Duke of York say he was
the rightful heir to the crown?

Peter. That my master was? No, forsooth: my master said
that he was, and that the King was an usurer.

Queen An usurper, thou wouldst say.

Peter Ay, forsooth, an usurper.

                                              (I.3.16–32)

Suffolks tears up the supplications, and Margaret dismisses the
petitioners as "base cullions" (40), but they seize upon Peter's
fumbling accusation to use against York to prevent him from
being assigned the regentship of France. The mistakes of the lower
class's language create both laughter and social commentary. The
first "supplication" points to abuses by the aristocracy and the
clientage system of powerful noblemen; the second to the tragedy
for the lower classes in the appropriation and enclosure of common
land used for grazing. The casualness with which such wrongs are
shrugged off tends to strengthen their claim to valid dissent, and
Peter's malapropism is no verbal mistake: Henry has promised
Suffolk a "fifteenth" to cover the expense of bringing Margaret
from France (I.1.132; in Part 1 Henry had levied a tax of a tenth
on personal property, V.5.93). Henry is more of a usurer than a
usurper, imposing heavy taxes to pay for a worthless marriage.
Either term challenges Henry's legitimacy and his self-conception
as a Christian ruler, and the pun parodies the ceremony of politics
by diminishing the capacity to name and confer status to an
armorer's apprentice's illiteracy. That Margaret and Suffolk should
appropriate such a flimsy piece of gossip to use against a nobleman
further reduces the dignity of the Court, though at the same time
it singles York out as potentially the most formidable opponent
among the eight aristocrats introduced in the opening scene.[13]

   The petitioners' objections are quietly forgotten as the scene turns
to the farce of Margaret's dropping her fan, ordering the Duchess
of Gloucester to pick it up, and boxing the kneeling Eleanor upon
the ear. When the discussion turns to "commonwealth affairs"

and the regentship, Horner and Peter once again interrupt the proceedings (which have quickly degenerated into angry insults anyway). Henry defers judgment to Gloucester, who reverses himself about regentship (compare I.3.160 and 205) and appoints a day for single combat between Peter and Horner. Ironically, by extending the chivalric practice of trial by combat to an armorer and his apprentice, Gloucester empties it of meaning and sets up what will be a grotesque parody of aristocratic values.[14] However much Henry values his uncle as a loyal counsellor, Duke Humphrey has been duped and magnifies a trivial occasion into a farcical inversion of dignity, chivalry, and justice. Along with his choleric insults, sumptuary excess, and silence about his wife's ambition, Gloucester's reversal about the regentship and his folly in dealing with these commoners compromise his pretensions to be the wise and judicious Lord Protector.

When the two combatants return to fight it out in the royal hall of justice, the audience is ready to expect great fun. The farce begins with the quite drunk Horner and his neighbors entering at one door and Peter and the quite drunk 'prentices at the other, both warriors equipped with staffs and sandbags.[15] The trial is over almost as soon as it has begun: Peter kills his master! The farce has turned grim and sour, as these simple men, terrified and drunk, act out a grotesque distortion of aristocratic formality; the laughter of an amusing interlude has turned into a farcically horrible death of an artisan (whose goods ironically provide his betters with the accoutrements of war and tourney) at the hands of his own apprentice. Horner, a simple man unwittingly involved in Suffolk's double machinations, both in deflecting the protest against his enclosing land and in attacking York, has been felled by a sandbag. As one commoner kills off another and in the process advances the interests of the nobleman, the exploitation of class is clearly and tellingly visualized in this travesty of chivalric encounter. Horner's dying confession of treason (II.3.91) seems ludicrous, and the onstage responses radically and even perhaps comically incongruous:

> *York* Take away his weapon. Fellow, thank God, and the good wine in thy master's way.
> *Peter* [kneeling.] O God! have I overcome mine enemies in this presence? O Peter! thou hast prevailed in right.
> *King* Go, take hence that traitor from our sight;

For by his death we do perceive his guilt:
And God in justice hath reveal'd to us
The truth and innocence of this poor fellow . . .

(92–100)

Henry's piety, credulity, and obliviousness to the reality of the
situation seems as callous as York's flippancy, and both add to
the kind of grotesque comedy which intensifies the darkness of
the play. Suffolk's little scheme has succeeded, but perhaps York
has learned something about the usefulness of manipulating the
commons; clearly, the Cade rebellion recapitulates this exploitation
on a larger scale.

In this context of grotesque comedy, the lengthy Simpcox scene
requires some brief attention. Again, the ordinary world bursts in
upon the courtly party, interrupting another exchange of insults
among the noblemen, bringing extraordinary news of a miracle
performed at the nearby shrine of Saint Alban's. It illustrates
Gloucester shrewdly and goodnaturedly handling the charlatan
Simpcox, thereby usefully serving his king, endearing himself to
the common people, and bolstering his self-conception as the wise
humanist judge. It provides the audience with a few good laughs
and gains sympathy for Gloucester, who is to be killed in the
next act. Perhaps more important than the unmasking of Saunder
Simpcox's "miracle" are the responses of the onstage audience of
Gloucester's exposure. The mayor and his brethren sarcastically cry
"A miracle!" The beadle "with whips" beats Simpcox over the head
and chases him offstage. Henry, whose faith had been confirmed
by Saint Alban's power, responds with an absurd lament: "O God,
see'st thou this, and bearest so long?" And Margaret comments as
the simple spectator: "It made me laugh to see the villain run"
(II.1.143–48). The Simpcoxes' charade, however, in a small way
also foreshadows the Cade rebellion, which, though anarchic, has
some basis in social discontent; "Alas, sir," she pleads, "we did it for
pure need" (150). Gloucester wants them "whipp'd through every
market-town, Till they come to Berwick, from whence they came"
(151–52), a punishment rather excessive in its severity. The scene
now turns back to the sophomoric and choleric animosity among
the Court:

Cardinal   Duke Humphrey has done a miracle to-day.

Suffolk   True, made the lame to leap and fly away.
Gloucester   But you have done more miracles than I:
You made in a day, my lord, whole towns to fly.

(159–62)

Buckingham at this point arrives with revenge for this insult, the news of Eleanor's traffic with spirits and "conspiracy" against "King Henry's life and death" (167). The Simpcox affair is thus sandwiched between angry name-calling and sarcasm and bracketed by the pastoral calm of the royal couple's hawking and the imminent threat of Gloucester's deposition as Lord Protector, further augmenting Henry's nightmare and farcically parodying the providential powers of religion with a false miracle followed by reports of necromancy.

Act IV escalates the violence into a full-scale and macabre dance-of-death, a nightmarish world in which the killings are multiplied and severed heads – Suffolk's (IV.4), Say's and Cromer's (IV.7), and Cade's (V.1) – punctuate the bloody anarchy. Like the Peter-Horner sequence, the Cade scenes begin in a mixture of nonsense, social discontent, and laughable farce and soon turn savagely brutal. Producing 2 *Henry VI* for the Oregon Shakespeare Festival in 1954, James Sandoe wrote of his audiences:

> Their response to the Cade scenes was distinct: they began by laughing as we all suspected but thereafter the ferocity of Cade and the little sprawl of mob caught their fun in the throat and turned it sour, especially as the second scene culminated in the harrowing of Lord Say and his haling offstage to be brought back (a head on a pike) an instant later, the mob growling and giggling madly . . . . The Simpcox sequence allows them one or two clear laughs, but Cade only lets them begin so, then bottles them up in horror.[16]

The ridiculous genealogy, the mock-nobility, the bombastic heroism, these are at first amusing, and Dick the Butcher's running commentary adds to the laughter, but Cade's rebellion becomes viciously and indiscriminately savage when the Clerk of Chatham is led offstage to be hanged for his literacy and Lord Say to be beheaded for speaking Latin. "O brave!" shout Cade's men, when the heads of Say and his son-in-law are brought in on pikes; Cade mockingly insists upon displaying them in a histrionic one-upmanship of grotesque military leadership:

> But is not this braver? Let them kiss one another; for they loved well when they were alive. Now part them again, lest they consult about the giving up of some more towns in France. Soldiers, defer the spoil of the city until night; for with these borne before us, instead of maces, will we ride through the streets; and at every corner have them kiss. Away! (IV.7.124–30)

Is not this braver? Courage has become butchery, defended through a parody of righteous, patriotic anger at the present administration's loss of Henry V's conquest in France. A more horrid image seems difficult to imagine for the ruling class's anxiety about the sinister and mindless potentiality for revolt among the have-nots and masterless men of London, yet this threat of apocalyptic slaughter is mixed with an open suggestion of aristocratic guilt in the military disasters abroad.[17] The Cade scenes cannot be taken simply as a dramatization of fears of what discontent might become – the mindless class hatred of the rude multitudes – for even here, in the most excessive and ludicrous of Cade's actions, there remains an objection with a legitimate basis in truth. Moreover, this speech offers one of many possible examples that direct us to an illuminating approach to Cade's antics: he is a parodic imitation and exaggeration of the equally irresponsible, haughty, and lawless noblemen whom he wishes to displace.

Very plausibly, Shakespeare makes York the instigator of Cade's rising – a connection absent from his sources – and it is York whom Cade most directly parodies. York himself has explained his plan in the self-satisfied soliloquy in which he glories in the good "fortune" of the Cardinal's assigning him an army to repress the rebellion of the "uncivil kerns of Ireland" (III.1.309–10). He has "seduc'd" Cade to "make commotion, as full well he can, Under the title of John Mortimer" and draw the "commons' mind" to "affect the house and claim of York" (355–75). While York is in Ireland, "This devil here shall be my substitute" (371). No one is fooled, as Shakespeare deliberately makes clear in the first scene of the Cade sequence by having William Stafford perceive the master schemer behind the accomplice's rebellion: "Jack Cade, the Duke of York hath taught you this" (IV.2.147). Cade's energy and vitality imitate York's, and his blustering leadership parodically reveals his teacher. Like his patron, Cade elaborates his royal lineage as John Mortimer (IV.2.37–50), just as York had (II.2.9–51); he calls Henry "usurper" (IV.4.29), just as Horner reports York had; he will rid England of "false caterpillars" and "sweep the court clean" (IV.4.36; IV.7.29), just as York promises to do (II.2.68–75); he exults in his military prowess and courage, just as York does; his hatred of literacy and cultural accomplishment exaggerates York's detestation of Henry's "bookish rule" (I.1.260). Cade's arrogance and unbridled violence clearly mirror York's singlemindedness, as does his willingness to face out the truth and the law with the naked assertion of the power of the sword. Even Cade's followers mock his pretensions to noble birth behind his back, deflating his claims with asides which reveal the disparity of fiction and reality. York and Cade are but two faces of the same lawless disorder which murders whatever lies in its path, and making Cade York's instrument significantly complicates the audience's response.

Cade's character and antics originate in the popular festivities of carnivalesque inversion which turned the world upside down during periods of holiday release.[18] York himself identifies Cade as a fantastic morris-dancer engaged in an entertaining sport of mock-battle and as a master of disguise and imitation:

> I have seen
> Him caper upright like a wild Morisco,
> Shaking the bloody darts as he his bells.
> Full often, like a shag-hair'd crafty kern,
> Hath he conversed with the enemy,
> And undiscover'd come to me again,
> And given me notice of their villanies.
> (III.1.364–70)

The comedy of such ritual practices of the mock-genres of folk festival pervades 2 Henry VI and provides an approach for describing the nature of its combination of farce and savagery. At the least violent extreme, the Simpcox scene presents a mock-miracle which ends with exposure and a slapstick beating of the impostor. The Peter-Horner sequence mocks the formal entrances of the tourney and proceeds to a mock-testament and a mock-battle with mock-weapons. The Cade scenes presents mock-processions, mock-triumphs, mock-knightings, totally inverting the world as it usually defines itself, mocking the pretensions of learning, order, and rule, just as was permitted by the freedoms of Carnival, May Day, Midsummer's Night, and various harvest festivals. Shakespeare's audience would have been familiar with these holiday sports, their forms and genres of enacting the high spirits released in turning the world upside down and inside out; for a day the powerful and the powerless exchange places: masters and servants, bishops and acolytes, the mighty and the humble, the rulers and the ruled. But if the forms of parody and inversion are borrowed from popular, carnivalesque festivity, Part 2's imitation of the licensed disorder of holiday sports turns its comic violence into savage farce. The forms violence takes are the mock-forms of Carnival, but the deaths are not pretense.

The conventions of carnivalesque inversion provide the language of anarchy in the Cade sequence. Jack Cade celebrates himself as a lord of misrule, making an incredible farrago of promises: the Land of Cockaigne, the repeal of enclosures, and universal brotherhood:

> Be brave then; for your captain is brave, and vows reformation. There shall be in England seven half-penny loaves sold for a penny; the three-hoop'd pot shall have ten hoops; and I will make it felony to drink small beer. All the realm shall be in common, and in Cheapside shall my palfrey go to grass. And when I am king, as king I will be . . . there shall be no money; all shall eat and drink on my score, and I will apparel them all in one livery, that they may agree like brothers, and worship me their lord. (IV.2.61–72)

Cade's self-cancelling illogic and illiteracy next lead to the execution of the Clerk of Chatham for being named "Emmanuel" and being able to write his name. Then, as Cade kneels and knights himself "Sir John Mortimer," the stage presents us with a visual parody of the power of naming (a very important royal prerogative) and of man's capacity for self-creation through heroic assertion (an imitation of York's ambition).

Thus, Cade's rebellion begins with delightfully comic parody, mockery, and nonsense mixed with both genuine social protest against the inequities of the law, the asymmetry of resources, and the exploitation of the poor and the grotesque horror of slaughtering the innocent. Dressing himself in the armor of the Sir Humphrey Stafford, whom his men have killed, Cade again presents a stage image of the ease with which violence legitimizes power by appropriating its symbolic forms. The outrageousness of Cade's accusations against Lord Say delights us through their ludicrous exaggeration, but his case against the ideological oppression of the humanist educator cannot be simply dismissed as blustering idiocy:

> Thou has most traitorously corrupted the youth of the realm in erecting a grammar-school; and whereas, before, our forefathers had no other books but the score and tally, thou hast caus'd printing to be us'd; and contrary to the King his crown, and dignity, thou hast built a paper-mill. It will be prov'd to thy face that thou hast men about thee that usually talk of a noun, and a verb, and such abominable words as no Christian ear can endure to hear. Thou has appointed justices of the peace, to call poor men before them about matters they were not able to answer. Moreover, thou has put them in prison; and because they could not read, thou hast hang'd them; when, indeed, only for that cause they have been most worthy to live. (IV.7.30–44)

Lord Say has richly clothed his horse, "when honester men than thou go in their hose and doublets" (49).

Yet the strength of Cade's vigorous defense of the ignorant and the poor is compromised by the mindless destruction of his mob in the streets of a burning London and by that mob's reduction of its wants to killing the lawyers and enjoying limitless quantities of beer and maidenheads. Cade is the grotesque nightmare of the aristocracy, a nightmare fueled – it seems implied – by anxiety that the rebels' "class hatred" may be fully justified. When Old Clifford and Buckingham call upon Cade's followers to renounce him, honor the memory of Henry V, and receive full pardons, Cade rallies them:

> I thought you would never have given out these arms till you had recover'd your ancient freedom; but you are all recreants and dastards, and delight to live in slavery to the nobility. Let them break your backs with burdens, take your houses over your heads, ravish your wives and daughters before your faces. (IV.8.25–31)

The violence is finally defused by Old Clifford's again reminding them of the glories of Henry V, adding threats of a French invasion, and conjuring up a new conquest of France. The rebels are swayed by this cynical and irrelevant fiction, and Cade takes to his heels. He meets his end in Alexander Iden's garden in Kent, as Shakespeare again emphasizes the centrality of the law in the ordering of human affairs. Iden kills a common thief and rude invader of his property, in self-defense and in protection of the "small inheritance" his father left him.[19] Cade's words themselves stress the violation of the law:

> [*Aside.*] Here's the lord of the soil come to seize me for a stray, for entering his fee-simple without leave.
> (IV.10.24–25).

Iden reluctantly fights a nameless madman who only informs him that he is Cade as he is dying.

The Iden scene, another of Shakespeare's inventions, reduces Cade's rebelliousness to simple hunger and exposes the impotence of leadership without followers; it also provides a quick dramatization of the intrusion of anarchy into the a-political squirarchy of the provinces. In the streets of London there had been no escape from polarization:

> *Stafford*   And you that be the King's friends, follow me.
> *Cade*   And you that love the commons, follow me.
> (IV.2.174–75)

This Kentish garden offers no safety from the violence of lawless men, however well intentioned Iden's Virgilian contentment:

> Lord! who would live turmoiled in the court,
> And may enjoy such quiet walks as these?
> This small inheritance my father left me
> Contenteth me, and worth a monarchy.
> I seek not to wax great by others' waning,
> Or gather wealth I care not with what envy:
> Sufficeth, that I have maintains my state,
> And sends the poor well pleased from my gate.
> (IV.10.16–23)

Moreover, this pretty speech is soon undermined by Iden's smug acceptance of his good fortune in the accident that has sent him Cade: his honor will be "emblazed" as he bears Cade's head "in triumph to the King" (70, 81–82), an expectation of profit fulfilled as he is knighted and rewarded with a "thousand marks" and a place in the Court he had despised (V.1.78–80).[20] The scene, therefore, presents us with the reality of sanity and order only to withdraw the possibility.

Clearly, Shakespeare intends that 2 *Henry VI* make his audience uncomfortable, and within the dramatic limits of this play there is no end to the audience's nightmare. Its comedy furthers the darkening of the ruthlessly violent political history, as the macabre stage images of killings and severed heads repeat themselves and stifle laughter with horror. Though to an Elizabethan spectator familiar with the fearsome brutality of public executions and with the carnivalesque atmosphere which often surrounded them, such dramatizations of the grotesque may have been less shocking, their violence seems deliberately intensified by the comic elements which are interspersed with them. The nightmarish world of 2 *Henry VI* does not permit complacency but provokes a reassessment of the relationship of ethics and politics: "Priests pray for enemies," says York's son Richard, the natural heir of his father's viciousness and ambition, "but princes kill" (V.2.71). We have yet to hear the Crookback's demonic laughter, but the Yorks' success threatens to make most orthodox political theory obsolete. On the other hand, by dramatizing the anarchy of the Wars of the Roses, the play exposes fears and anxieties that threaten to control us the more they are left unexpressed; by conjuring up the dark and demonic side of politics, it creates the discomfort which is too readily suppressed.

Finally, the carnivalesque elements involved in the comic sequences suggest considering the play itself as promoting the kind of release Carnival provided. After all, theater is the art of illusion, and presumably the actors of Shakespeare's company are revived at the end of Act V to receive the applause of the spectators. The entire play has been an illusion of multiple deaths and beheadings, just as the mockeries of popular festivals had re-enacted spectacles of pretended killing. The play's radically aggressive and horribly grotesque violence ends at last, and we can sigh with relief and return to business as usual. In 2 *Henry VI*, however, the demons have been invoked but not subdued or exorcised. Within the Saturnalian world of inversions and reversals, lawlessness is the norm; with such folk festivals and popular diversions on the wane in post-Reformation England, the theater itself was becoming a substitute for these forms of entertainment.[21] No doubt, there is earnestness in Shakespeare's sport with the bloodiness of English history and an awareness of the hostility of class such carnivalesque practices freely and openly expressed, however persuasive the safety-valve theory of Carnival may seem. "Alas! sir, we did it for pure need," laments Simpcox's wife (II.1.150), and without such dramatic contrasts of rich and poor in Lancastrian or Elizabethan England, the Wat Tylers, Jack Cades, and rioters of the 1590s would have no followers. The play ultimately is deeply ambivalent about the discontent of the rude multitude, allowing the stage to provide a site for ideological contest amidst an anarchy which insures that England will suffer from the conflict.

The contemporaneity of 2 *Henry VI* must have been more readily apparent to its original audiences, yet the elements of topical significance do more to extend the geography and felt life of the social drama of the English history play than to address the problems toward which they point. The Irish were once again rebellious in the 1590s, yet York's excursion to put down the "uncivil kerns" is given brief space, an incidental plot strand which offers him an unforeseen opportunity to gather a large army for his political ambitions. Food riots were common in the early 1590s, yet in Cade's wild utopian fantasies the reality of scarcity and hunger among the poor is overshadowed by the crazy demogoguery and anarchic, iconoclastic violence. Enclosures had been and would continue to be a factor in the social discontent among the rural lower classes, yet the play does little more than raise the topic. The accumulation of these subversive causes for rebellion among the powerless, however, pervades the play, and it does dramatize the potentiality for exerting influence and demanding a place upon the stage of politics within collective action. The commons effectively demand Suffolk's dismissal from Henry's court, making the King bow to their threats. Even if Cade is York's factotum, he does burn half of London and temporarily commands London Bridge; gruesome as his killings are, they do illustrate the ease with which such an uprising can achieve a following and immediate success. Finally, Cade becomes the Lord of Misrule dethroned, a kind of Jack o' Lent ritually driven out as Shrove Tuesday turns into Ash Wednesday, though he fits the scapegoat pattern only formally and not ideologically. The concerns of the commoners are presented as heartfelt discontent with their treatment at the hands of the exploitative nobility, as motivated by real inequities and injustices. If Cade's outrages become disturbingly vile and murderous, the plausible dissent expressed is not simply cancelled, nor the status quo defended. Whatever the violence of mob psychology, the asymmetries of class warrant political action. The stage has given voice – as formerly the inversions of carnivalesque folk festivals had – to expectations of legitimacy, proportionality, and justice in the distribution of resources and to challenges to authority when those expectations are violated. The anxiety evoked by Cade's horrors cannot mastered by Iden's "heroism"; instead, it merely finds itself subsumed within the greater social pathology of the Wars of the Roses. Cade represents, no doubt, the demonization of the rebellious peasant, but the commons will not accept and do not deserve their space at the margins of history.

4

Henry VI, Part Three

THE LAW OF THE SCABBARD

After Jack Cade's barbaric destructiveness in Part 2, a bloodier and more anarchic sequel seems at first unimaginable, but as Edgar in *King Lear* tells us, "The worst is not So long as we can say 'This is the worst'" (IV.1.28). From the entrance of the bloody Yorks to the on-stage murder of Henry VI, *3 Henry VI* relentlessly explores "the worst": the absolute nadir of the English past, the grotesque brutalities of the War of the Roses. The law of the scabbard leads to the bloodbath of a civil war, not only with the inevitability of a cynical power politics of naked force but also with a metaphysical certainty through which the actively destructive energies of chaos reveal their own perverted (and even in its own way artistic) compulsion to shatter all bonds of order.[1] Not simply a passive condition in which order is absent nor a totally unpredictable and unheeding urge to set all things at strife, chaos forms part of the paradoxical metaphysics of the natural and the social mystery, and its energies cause the absoluteness with which we regard the oppositions of order/anarchy, natural/unnatural, and so on to collapse upon themselves. In political terms, the dogs of war have been unleashed and there's no getting them back into the kennel; in physical terms, man is carried along in his precarious existence by the gales and tides of fortune's tempests.

In Henry VI's image, the political is compared to the natural, both of which are at war with themselves:

> This battle fares like to the morning's war,
> When dying clouds contend with growing light,
> What time the shepherd, blowing of his nails,
> Can neither call it perfect day nor night.
> Now sways it this way, like a mighty sea

Forc'd by the tide to combat with the wind;
Now sways it that way, like the self-same sea
Forc'd to retire by fury of the wind.
Sometime the flood prevails, and then the wind;
Now one the better, then another best;
Both tugging to be victors, breast to breast;
Yet neither conqueror nor conquered.
So is the equal poise of this fell war.
(II.5.1–13)

The contention spells the way of the world; nothing stands still and all changes and there really emerge no victors, only combatants caught in sportive struggle of winds and waves, which are themselves combatants. Margaret's long speech in Act V uses the storm-tossed ship as a metaphor for her condition, repeating Henry's sense of hopelessness but exhorting her followers to courageously battle the ruthless elements rather than sit still and lament. Oxford, Somerset, and her son, Prince Edward, praise her valiant and resolute spirit, yet Margaret's comparisons of the Yorks to the elemental forces of nature underline how doomed their struggle is (V.4.1–37). Margaret's image connects the Yorks with the primordial, elemental, nonhuman, destructive power of nature; avoiding such a power is impossible and opposing it is futile. The storm-tossed ship provides as well an image of the groundlessness of political action, a groundlessness concisely expressed later in Richard's mockery of pity, love, fear, and all "which greybeards call divine" (V.6.81). Authority is sheathed in the scabbard, whose "law" is man's imitation of the destructive energies of nature.

The play sets out – almost programmatically – to destroy every vestige of man-made order, as the Yorks challenge and violate the ceremonial, formal, liturgical, and familial bonds of civilized living, forcing as they do the violent revenges of the Lancasters and their followers. *3 Henry VI* is a drama of mutilation, its stage filled with severed heads, dead bodies, heads on gates, paper crowns, bloody armor, bloody swords, bloody handkerchiefs. Its opening speeches set the tone: the bloody Yorks boasting of their killings, Richard exposing the severed head of Somerset. Look what we have done, cry his sons Richard and Edward, as the father proceeds to assume possession of the English throne, his right by the strength of naked force. The Yorks become from the beginning predators in this jungle of politics; they literally storm the stage, invading the theater, scaling the balcony to occupy the visually superior position above the king who enters below, stage-directing their soldiers to take up their guard on the stage of politics. Shakespeare clearly dramatizes this aspect of the theatricality of the political and follows it by having the triumphant Duke of York force his own interpretation of legitimacy upon the impotent king and his loyal nobles, a version of history and law which it matters little whether they accept or not, since the battlefield remains the ultimate arena for settling such disputes.

York is placated by Henry's disinheriting his son and making him the heir of the kingdom, but in the next scene his sons persuade him to break his oath of loyalty to the king and again assume the throne. The dramatic pattern has been clearly drawn: the normal expectations of the son's inheriting his father's title, of the action's following a sworn pledge, of the law's governing the nation, all are overthrown. The head is severed from the body, the crown from the king, the word from its meaning; parliament is made a shambles, the queen shall lead an army, revenge has replaced justice, ritual has been emptied of its power. All connections are broken, and individual actions seem like the violent ricochets of Lucretian atoms in a world of strife. Shakespeare has swiftly established the horror of this world: the Yorks' gloating and relish of violence and mutilation (I.1. 1–20); Clifford's murder of young Rutland (I.3); Margaret's and Clifford's taunting the dying Duke of York (I.4). Atrocity becomes a source of pleasure. Revenge and self-interest govern politics and civil war, distorting the traditional bonds of state and even family – it sometimes becomes difficult to remember who killed whom in retaliation for the death of what butchered relative – and ultimately destroying any common basis of humanity. After experiencing Terry Hands' productions of all the Henry VI plays, David Daniell concluded: "Anyone can now do anything to anyone, it seems. The spectator is made to concentrate on a physical landscape with fewer and fewer figures, who go wearily through fewer and fewer possibilities: but the mental landscape is without boundaries at all, and this enervated world is violent in its fantasies."[2] Effacing those boundaries well describes Part Three's plot.

The isolation which results from aggressive self-interest produces disastrous consequences for those unfortunate enough to tossed about by the gales and waves of anarchy. Isolated from his followers, Henry VI falls an easy prey to Richard's murderousness. The three York brothers are re-united in the final ensemble scene, but their unity is obviously tenuous, fractured by Clarence's defection and return and by Edward's folly in taking Lady Grey as his queen; the Yorkist victory hardly spells order in family or nation. Richard lies in waiting for both brothers.

The visual and verbal imagery for this chaos centers around the bloodliness of battle and murder, but in terms of the politics of *3 Henry VI* Shakespeare has moved the actors in this dramatization of English history beyond ideology. Among other things, ideology is the system of representations through which the political life of the nation is given continuity and coherence. Those representations are radically undermined in the play's insistent mockery and parody of the forms ideological practice assumes in the normal everyday workings of government, and the next section analyzes some of these inversions and mutilations of form in detail. At this point in the discussion, we may look at two aspects of the overall structuring of discontinuity and incoherence: the almost liturgical scene of the Father who has killed his son and the Son who has killed his father (II.5) and the play's great opposites in characterization, Henry VI and Richard Crookback.

The Son–Father scene in a rather emblematic way dramatizes the disorder of civil war; stylistically, it appears out of place, an intrusion of the almost purely symbolic, but theatrically it has always revealed an effectiveness beyond the reader's expectations. The scene puzzled Sir Barry Jackson at first; preparing to direct Part Three in 1952, he considered it one of his most difficult problems:

> Though we know that family cleavages of such a tragic nature occurred in Germany during our lifetime and that the parricides were not even accidental, Shakespeare's directions, when read, easily raise a smile. Rather than run the risk of a laugh in the audience, we discussed omitting the incident altogether. The poet's infallible intuition, however, proved right. The scene was retained, but treated as a static tableau: it shone out away and above the violent episodes with which it is surrounded and threw more light on the horror of civil war than all the scenes of wasteful bloodshed. The still figures of the father and son speaking quietly and unemotionally, as though voicing the the thoughts that strike the saintly, sad King's

conscience, presented a moment of calm and terrible reflection.[3]

Again, in 1977 under Terry Hands' direction the scene produced powerful responses in its audiences.[4]

The level of symbolic abstraction is unusual even for early Shakespeare, but the scene accomplishes a complexity beyond the antiphonal bereavement of the two unnamed soldiers and beyond their representativeness as common Englishmen caught in the ugliness of dynastic revenge. Life has been stripped of any continuity: the single combats of the battlefield are meaningless episodes not part of a coherent struggle between causes or even historical forces; the combatants have lost even any identity; the anonymity of the dead cruelly reveals a Lucretian universe of randomly directed atoms. The War of the Roses becomes absolutely insignificant politically or ideologically, as the utter lucidity of the scene brings home to the simplest theatergoer the most extreme lessons of the darkly ironic situation. The clarity is blinding, and there can be no explanations for the multitude of family tragedies these two stand for. All this sorrow is set within the pastoral conventions with which the scene begins, as the "gentle" king laments the discords of war and longs for a shepherd's life; ironically he sits upon the stage "molehill" which figured prominently in York's death, a few scenes previously. The same field may be used for battle or for pasture; the molehill for mockery or for the meditation which foreshadows death for Henry. Both Son and Father drag their victims onstage, and the first thoughts of both are to plunder the slain, look for crowns and gold. Both searches immediately lead to the tragic recognition, and greed gives way to grief, repentance, calling upon God to pardon and to pity these deeds, and remembering the mother and wife who must soon learn of these deaths. The mutilation of every human value could hardly be more concisely distilled.

The two characters who stand back from this general mayhem of civil war and understand it the most thoroughly are Henry VI and Richard of Gloucester. Henry's detachment, religious and moral, finally comes to represent the anti-political approach to the actively destructive energies of chaos; Richard's detachment, intelligent and theatrical, emerges as a recognition of the groundlessness of politics and the freeplay which its discontinuities allow the clever man to invent discrete and manipulable episodes and scenes on the stage of politics, to harness those destructive energies for his own benefit rather than be driven by them and eventually become their victim, as has happened or will happen to all the others.

Henry's powerlessness in making peace in Part Two is replaced by retreat in Part Three; the gentle king would prefer the life of low content, far from the imbroglios of civil war, free from "Fortune's spite" (IV.6.19). Most often his impotence and final unwillingness to participate in the power politics appears a weakness in character, but Shakespeare often enough suggests that that reluctance has been hard-won and might be regarded as strength of character. He comes to accept "sour adversity," to acknowledge his unfitness for the kingly role, to achieve a mature confidence that his failures may unking him but not unman him; he explains his identity to his "keepers":

> More than I seem, and less than I was born to:
> A man at least, for less I should not be;
> And men may talk of kings, and why not I? . . . .
> My crown is in my heart, not on my head;
> Not deck'd with diamonds and Indian stones,
> Not to be seen: my crown is called content;
> A crown it is that seldom kings enjoy.
>   (III.1.56–58, 62–65)

Henry becomes in Part Three a choric figure, but also a much more human character. He is appalled by the violence but also educated by it. For the warring nobles the iconicity of kingship means nothing; for the common man the king has only iconic value, and it matters not what particular man is king since his allegiance is only to kingship. Shakespeare has discovered the doubleness of the king's role: as the king, Henry remains the weak and often comic character of the first two parts; as a man, Henry grows in self-knowledge and strength as he gains a secure sense of his own values, a surer faith in the absolutes which have served him so poorly in the political world, and a more profound understanding of his own humanity. As king, he fails; as a man, he rests secure in God's grace.

Henry's Christianity gives him that strength and also provides him with his only way of making sense of this radically discontinuous world. The religious perspective makes all men equal as God's sinners and children and gives Henry the power of prophesying a better future; "Come hither, England's hope," he commands the young Richmond:

> If secret powers
> Suggest but truth to my divining thoughts,
> This pretty lad will prove our country's bliss.
> His looks are full of peaceful majesty,
> His head by nature fram'd to wear a crown,
> His hand to wield a sceptre, and himself
> Like to bless in time a regal throne.
> Make much of him, my lords; for this is he
> Must help you more than you are hurt by me.
>   (IV.6.68–76)

Only faith – a certainty about the coherence and continuity of history from a divine perspective – can give him such assurance, as such a prediction seems comically disproportionate to the circumstances present in the historical moment.

If Henry VI responds to the nihilistic world of the War of the Roses with Christian faith and resignation, Richard of Gloucester perceives the opportunities provided by the fragmentation of order and the absence of ideology. Since every moment has become a discrete episode unconnected to the past or to contemporaneous incidents, since mask and face, role and identity, word and action, ritual and meaning, have been severed, the master of the art of acting will become the master of politics. The severing of connections produces Henry's alienation, and it is painful to lose wife, son, and subjects, but his religiosity will compensate for and overcome his isolation. For Richard, the isolation is desirable and a source of power in itself: "I have no brother . . . I am myself alone" (V.6.80,83). Even with all the vengeful brutalities of the play, the same dissociation of family ties and isolation might be attributed to almost any of the characters, forswearers, oath-breakers, turncoats, self-seekers, and betrayers as they all are. But only Richard declares his independence self-consciously and makes dissimulation complement fraud in his deliberate plans to gain the crown. He will profit from the anarchy and sow more violence and discord; that's his genius and that's the new discovery of Part Three.

Henry VI discovers that a man may be a man apart from his socially assigned role; Richard understands that a man may play all roles and not be discovered, since the radical discontinuities created in a world without political ethics and without even the certainty of family loyalties fragment the play of politics into separate scenes in which the consistency of the performance will produce the momentarily persuasive gesture, identity, and shape for the occasion. His machiavellian father had managed to use Cade and his discontents to further the Yorkist cause, a clever enough ruse but one difficult to control, one unlikely to succeed more than once, one easily seen through and squelched. Richard plans to discipline the anarchy and violence, to manage it, to create an almost infinitely variable methodology for succeeding. He will be "himself alone" yet "frame" his performance to "all occasions" (III.2.185). J. P. Brockbank's observation provides a useful sense of Richard's "character" as partly a sum of the others' less conscious and more "single" identities:

> Richard not only reacts to events (all the barons do that) he also becomes the conscious embodiment of all the drives – moral, intellectual, and physical – that elsewhere show themselves only in the puppetry. Translating into theatrical terms, we might say that when he takes the stage for his first exercise of the soliloquy prerogative he inherits from York (at the end of III.ii), his language shows him capable of playing the part of York, Clifford, Edward, Margaret, or Warwick. All their energies are made articulate: the doggedness of York that "reaches at the moon" and the same eye for the glitter of the Marlovian crown; the dedication to Clifford which characterizes Clifford; the prurience of Edward; the decorated and ruthless rhetoric of Margaret; and Warwick's gifts of king-maker, resolute "to command, to check, to overbear."[5]

Richard not only embodies these energies of chaos, he also and alone of all these violent men and women fully believes he can discipline them to his service.

In this long soliloquy Richard outlines his desire to be king and the apparently insurmountable obstacles between himself and the crown, becoming more violently bound to his ambition as he studies the absense of alternatives and its difficulties, finally raising himself to a pitch of explosive desperation:

> And I, – like one lost in a thorny wood,
> That rents the thorns and is rent with the thorns,

> Seeking a way, and straying from the way,
> Not knowing how to find the open air,
> But toiling desperately to find it out –
> Torment myself to catch the English crown:
> And from that torment will I free myself,
> Or hew my way out with a bloody axe.
>
> (174–81)

The lack of discipline in this violent "seeking and straying" is self-destructive to his purposes; the following lines settle the frenzy and devise a controlled, deliberate approach to catching the crown:

> Why, I can smile, and murder whiles I smile,
> And cry 'Content!' to that that grieves my heart,
> And wet my cheeks with artificial tears,
> And frame my face to all occasions . . .
> I'll play the orator as well as Nestor,
> Deceive more slily than Ulysses could,
> And, like a Sinon, take another Troy.
> I can add colours to the chameleon,
> Change shapes with Proteus for advantages,
> And set the murderous Machiavel to school.
> Can I do this, and cannot get a crown?
> Tut! were it further off, I'll pluck it down.
>
> (182–95)

Mastering the arts of deception becomes the highest asset in the theater of politics and a self-conscious discipline essential in developing that artistry. But the conscience also must be disciplined, as the soliloquy clearly is meant to match Henry's previous meditations (II.5 and III.1). Henry internalizes the "crown": "My crown is in my heart . . . my crown is call'd content" (III.1.62, 64). Richard must "cry 'Content!' to that that grieves my heart" (III.2.183) and spies the crown far off. Part of that grief issues from Richard's physical deformity; he is not a "proper" man like his brother Edward and cannot pursue the amorous rites of love: the soliloquy follows his and Clarence's eavesdropping on Edward's wooing Lady Grey, and its first line – "Ay, Edward will use women honorably" – connects his ambition with his being cut off from fulfilling that role. Presumably, what grieves his heart is also the failure of the Yorkist cause as a family affair: Edward's folly with

Lady Grey demonstrates his complete lack of any understanding of the necessity to use the prerogatives of dynastic marriage astutely and substitutes the prerogative of the royal will for the wise management of the public symbols of kingly office. The lover's role and the brother's loyalty are effectively denied him as roles to play; that grieves him yet he will search out a role which will challenge his energies and which he can fulfil. The sense of struggle within Richard is not developed very thoroughly in the remainder of this play, but the conflict is here clearly established: the "torment" of frustrated ambition urges the suppression of the heart's grief over the alternatives denied him and the actions that ambition demands.

Unlike York or Clifford or Margaret, Richard clearly knows his deeds are morally perverse; only by disciplining his conscience and allying himself with the diabolical may he succeed in catching the crown. His speech after the murder of Henry returns to this imposed and disciplined mastery of conscience, as he disavows all brothers and exorcises all remnants of pity, love, and fear:

> And this word 'love,' which greybeards call divine,
> Be resident in men like one another
> And not in me: I am myself alone.
>
> (V.6.81–83)

How different this sounds from the other boastful murders; M. M. Reese comments: "Left alone with Henry's body, Gloucester blusters like a man with a bad conscience. Before he silenced them, Henry's words had hit their mark, and he shows the reactions of a guilty man."[6] Only with such an understanding of Richard can the audience perceive the full extent of the separateness of each individual produced by the anarchy of a political world beyond ideology.

RITUALIZING ATROCITY

In *3 Henry VI* Shakespeare further escalates the grotesque comedy of Part 2 by formalizing the violence, by ritualizing the atrocities and horrors of unrestrained ambition, and by turning the laughter against the audience. In producing the second and third parts of *Henry VI* at Birmingham in 1952, Sir Barry Jackson found that the line "between the risible and the serious is of such infinitesimal breadth that the reaction of the audience can never be foretold."[7] These kinds of difficulties of response begin with the first scene in Part 3: in the first few lines the York family exults in their victories at St. Alban's, the father boasting, Edward waving his bloody sword, and Richard crying

> Speak thou for me, and tell them what I did.
> [*Throwing down the Duke of Somerset's head.*]·
> (I.1.16)

His bouncing this severed head onto the floorboards of any stage is as likely to elicit laughter as it is shock. Later in the play, it would seem equally difficult not to enjoy Queen Margaret's mockery of the villainous York, as she places him on a molehill, crowns him with a paper coronet, and taunts him with malicious sarcasm (I.4), or not to relish the savage humor of the three York sons' stichomythic mock-eulogy over the dead Clifford (II.6), or not to smile at the asides of Richard and Clarence when brother Edward is trying to seduce Lady Grey in the most coarse, bawdy, and clumsy manner (III.2). The grisly comedy most often surpasses anything in the first two parts.

Several patterns emerge from the grim scenes in Part 3, the most obvious of which is the ritualization of the grotesque. In Part 1 the repetition of scenes of false reconciliation reveals an ironic discrepancy between appearances and intentions which makes politics a farce; in Part 2 the mock-ritual of a trial by combat leads from farcical drunkenness and sandbags and staffs to Horner's death, and Cade the mock-king dons Stafford's armor and leads a procession through London with the severed heads of Say and Cromer kissing at every corner. Ritual and ceremony become dramatic only when broken, challenged, violated, mocked, inverted, misapplied, parodied. Part 3 begins with a deliberate mockery of ceremony: York installs himself on the throne, and King Henry VI and his counsellors enter in what becomes almost the role of supplicants. York's arrogant daring stages the utmost in rebelliousness, as it visually echoes Lucifer's sitting on God's throne in the Chester cycle's *Fall of Lucifer*, and the staging stresses the reality of York's superior power by directing York and sons to ascend to the gallery and Henry and his party to enter below. Sheer power makes this usurpation possible; Richard asserts the authority of force in a comically sarcastic boast: "Sound drums and trumpets, and the King will fly" (118). Even Henry sees his powerlessness here, and his concern for the sanctity of ceremony thereby appears rather comically delicate:

> Far be the thought of this from Henry's heart,
> To make a shambles of the parliament-house!
> (70–71)

As in Part 2, Henry plays the blessed peacemaker: he disinherits his son and names York his successor on the condition that York take an oath to "cease this civil war" (203). The private quarrel between Henry and Margaret – husband and wife more than king and queen – dramatizes by contrast just how thoroughly the foregoing compromise and false reconciliation have inverted the ideals of chivalry, loyalty, royalty, and fatherhood.

This usurpation of ceremony not only seems a machiavellian necessity in the transition of sovereignty but also prepares the audience's emotional expectations for Margaret's revenge at Wakefield. Appropriately enough, the scene suggests the buffeting, interrogation, and scourging of Christ from the Wakefield Master's mystery cycle, though any number of medieval Passion plays include such elements of the torture and physical suffering surrounding the crucifixion. Margaret's revenge grotesquely parodies the basic structure of the Passion and mutilates as well familiar images of monarchy, humanity, knighthood, and fatherhood. "Anarchism," Brockback comments, "is more dramatic when it is iconoclastic."[8] The paper crowning creates a ceremony around this brutal murder, ritualizing the atrocity, and intensifying the venomous comedy of the chroniclers' accounts of the incident. Margaret has progressed a long way from the witty "quid for quo" of her exchanges with Suffolk in Part 1 (V.3.109), and her savage sarcasm, however much York has earned her hatred, is terrible in its exulting vengeance. The blasphemous analogy of York's paper crown to Christ's crown of thorns indicates the tone of the Queen's sardonic taunting. John Russell Brown's description of Dame Peggy Ashcroft's performance in this scene (Stratford, 1964) defines its effectiveness and the darkness of its parodic and macabre comedy:

> The cruel humour of the lines was played close to hysteria: 'I prithee grieve to make me merry' (line 86) was an almost

necessary request to excuse Margaret's impulse towards helpless
laughter, a physical and emotional relief and a breakdown of control. Margaret was constantly changing her stance and position
as if instinctively; her taunts were controlled and insistent so
that only her body, moving repeatedly, could show the inward
instability. As York replied in pain and passion, Margaret was
silent, after one last, and now forced, laugh. When she stabbed
him it was with a quick movement, and then she wept. And
then the tears stopped with a wild, painful cry. In this scene
the violence was emphasized as much as anywhere, but there
was also rhetorical and musical control and a daring, emotional
performance.[9]

This interpretation rings true: Margaret's passion has pushed her
beyond suffering into that Ovidian hysteria which also characterizes
Titus Andronicus. The ritualization of this excess makes it even more
theatrically grotesque, more shocking, more horrible, as Margaret
passes beyond what we usually recognize as human.

Comparison of this scene with the crude and perverse wit of
Marlowe readily discloses the greater complexity and sophistication
of Shakespeare's theatrical artistry; consider these examples of *The
Massacre at Paris's* dark humor:

> *Lord High Admiral*   O let me pray before I dye.
> *Gonzago*   Then pray unto our Ladye, kisse this crosse . . .
>   *Stab him.*

>   *   *   *

> *Loreine*   I am a preacher of the word of God.
> And thou a traitor to thy soule and him.
>   *Guise*   Dearly beloved brother, thus tis written . . .
>   *He stabs him.*

>   *   *   *

> *Seroune*   O Christ my Savior.
> *Mountsorrell*   Christ, villaine?
> Why darest thou to call on Christ,
> Without the intercession of some Saint?
>   *Sanctus Jacobus*   hee was my Saint, pray to him.
>   *Seroune*   O let me pray unto my God.
>   *Mountsorrell*   Then take this with you . . . *Stab him.*

The Massacre at Paris is a crude, mangled fragment, but the same sort of theatrical, dance-of-death humor can be found in Marlowe's other plays. The striking difference is in Shakespeare's development of an elaborate formality which complicates our response to the vileness of cold-blooded murder, of parodic perversion of sacred ritual which resonates with a more suggestive overlay of images and creates a tension among the possible emotional and interpretive responses of the spectator.

Ritualizing the atrocity makes Shakespeare's scene more effectively grotesque; carefully orchestrated, the excessive cruelty becomes not merely perversely comic but also more revolting in its ceremoniousness. Our ambivalent response is conditioned by the odd mixture of stylized rhetoric and colloquial insult, of ceremony and brutality, of humor and horror. The Yorks have their turn again at Towton, and again a mock-ritual – this time a parodic combination of eulogy and shriving – is blasphemously performed: the dead Clifford is offered confession for his sins:

> *Richard* Clifford, ask mercy, and obtain no grace.
> *Edward* Clifford, repent in bootless penitence.
> *Warwick* Clifford, devise excuses for thy faults.
> *George* While we devise fell tortures for thy faults.
> (II.6.69–72)

The effect of such inversions of liturgical ritual is to disorient the audience, to shock us out of our assurance that human psychology and conduct have certain fixed parameters; discomfort, insecurity, and anxiety are brought to the surface as we find ourselves plunged into a more and more savagely farcical world. The transformation of murder and blasphemy into ritual increases that anxiety, for the atrocities have been formalized and stylized into the ironic wit, elegant sarcasm, and sophisticated savagery of art and play. The laughter which should act as a kind of relief or defense-mechanism against brutality turns into revulsion, as the humor reveals horror also, yet the iconoclasm and energy exert a fascination if not an attraction which intensifies the ambivalence of response. Terry Hands found producing Part Three more difficult than the other two Henry VI plays, because it "goes off into ritual, in fact into terrible ceremonial where extreme savagery is balanced by extreme grief over it" and the "monstrous horror" by "ribald black humor."[10]

One might object to this sort of analysis by pointing to the comic horror as conventional and cite the Herods of the mysteries, the Vices of the moralities, and the Titanic monster-heroes of Marlowe, but to see one or all of these characters or personifications in the Yorks and Lancasters is not to dismiss the disturbing quality of the grotesque theatricality of *3 Henry VI*. Rather such connections intensify the nightmarishness of the play, as Shakespeare closes the aesthetic distance between stage and spectator by drawing upon these literary traditions for the history play and by making rituals of the mockery of people and politics. Consider, for example, how the saintly Henry becomes a sad but comic figure when all ignore his sovereignty and even his queen silences him. In II.2, for example, the Lancasters meet the Yorks before the town of York; Henry tries to interrupt the exchange of anger between Richard of Gloucester and Clifford:

> *K. Hen.*   Have done with words, my lords, and hear me speak.
> *Q. Mar.*   Defy them then, or else hold close thy lips.
> *K. Hen.*   I prithee give no limits to my tongue:
> I am a king, and privileg'd to speak.
> (II.2.117–20)

The necessity of a king's having to assert this regal privilege is comic enough but it also must be made against his wife's stage-directing his rhetoric. Moreover, Henry is effectively silenced, for he does not speak for the rest of the scene, a matter of almost sixty lines, and if the audience had not noticed the king's silence, Edward points out that Margaret "deniest the gentle king to speak" (172). The derision is placed *inside* the play, and the audience finds itself not only laughing *at* the characters who deserve scorn but laughing *with* the deriders on stage who mock them.

Edward's wooing of Lady Grey is another example. Richard and Clarence, apparently out of earshot of their conversation, comment upon their brother's crudeness and bluntness. They perceive the scene as a parodic mime of the ritualistic gestures of courtship; for the audience it is that and more: a ritualized bargaining to exchange Lady Grey's sons and lands for her chastity. The irony of Edward's having to seize her property and threaten her sons' lives in order to have anything to negotiate with deepens the sardonic tone, while Richard and Clarence encourage us to laugh at the scene. The brothers use the imagery with which they had mocked the dead Clifford –

> *Richard* [*Aside to George.*]
> The ghostly father now hath done his shrift.
> *George* [*Aside to Richard.*]
> When he was made a shriver, 'twas for shrift.
>
> (III.2.107–8)

In this way they link the anti-Lancaster sarcasm with their scorn for their own brother. The punning and comic rhyme point out the mockery of amatory ritual by comparing the scene with another ceremony, and the formality of Edward's wooing appears more grotesque, because the complex layers of mockery intensify the irony of a courtship already drastically coarsened in content.

In the next scene another amatory ritual is underway in the King of France's palace with Warwick's wooing of Lady Bona for Edward. Although neither grimaces nor guffaws are evoked here, the mockery of politics as a muddle of errors is clearly intended, as Margaret defends Henry's possession of the throne, insists upon the existence of his son (who stands beside her), and accuses Warwick of deceiving them all. The Post's message interrupts this parody of the rituals of diplomatic negotiation – itself as much a perversion of romantic ideas about love and marriage as Edward's gamesmanship with Lady Grey is – and completely upstages Warwick; Edward has duped the king-maker and his amatory broker. Hands calls the scene a "moment of strip cartoon": "In that horrid, grief-stricken, nightmarish world suddenly something strikes that is utterly zany."[11] Even Warwick directs the audience to understand this scene's perversion of politics: King Lewis declares war against Edward for "mocking marriage with a dame of France" (III.3.255), and Warwick vows vengeance in his scene-ending soliloquy:

> Then none but I hall turn his jest to sorrow.
> I was the chief that rais'd him to the crown.
> And I'll be chief to bring him down again:
> Not that I pity Henry's misery,
> But seek revenge on Edward's mockery.
>
> (261–65)

From this chaos of the the political jungle emerges the grand manipulator of all appearances, the Protean Richard Crookback.

Already characterized by his military brutality, sarcastic wit, and physical deformity, in the middle of 3 *Henry VI* he picks up the gleeful mockery of his Marlovian and machiavellian father and combines it with the wry satanism of the morality Vice. The painful and provocative element of comedy in a Tamburlaine arises from the radical discrepancy between reality and heroic rhetoric. Richard often sounds like a Tamburlaine or a Barabbas or a Guise or even a Faustus, and like Marlowe's heroes he fascinates audiences by his daring, cleverness, imagination, and resolve. Like the victims of Marlowe's protagonists, also, most of Richard's attract little sympathy, for they are merely moral weaklings as well as naive politicians. But this Shakespearean chameleon is more changeable than Marlowe's overreachers, and the effect – even in 3 *Henry VI* – of his ruthless viciousness and comic diabolism is more complex because of the multifaceted, histrionic self-dramatization of an actor who knows he is acting, tells us he is, and yet conceals his deceit from those onstage.

One must not, however, succumb to the temptation to conflate the last two acts of Part 3 with *Richard III*. The whirligig of battles and betrayals allows Richard little room to exercise his theatrical talents and comic virtuosity. Yet the soliloquy at the end of III.2 and the murder of Henry VI establish his commanding stage presence and provide the strong contrast with the gentle king which strongly indicates what we are to make of this nihilistic stretch of English history. Combined with the scenes in which the atrocities of bloody revenge and inhuman cruelty, the characters of Henry and Richard suggest the deep ambivalence with which we are to regard the nastiness of the War of the Roses.

If we are correct in asserting with Brockbank that "anarchism . . . is more dramatic when it is iconoclastic," it remains crucial to determine the relationship of anarchy, theater, iconoclasm, and ambivalence. On the one hand, the religious absolutes of King Henry have been revealed as irrelevant to the exercise of political power; political ethics are even a burden to the king who tries to govern through mercy, justice, and selfless care for his subjects; Henry himself spells this out even better than does Richard:

> I have not stopp'd mine ears to their demands,
> Nor posted off their suits with slow delays;
> My pity hath been balm to heal their wounds,
> My mildness hath allay'd their swelling griefs,

My mercy dried their water-flowing tears;
I have not been desirous of their wealth,
Nor much oppress'd them with great subsidies,
Nor forward of revenge, though they much err'd.
Then why should they love Edward more than me?
                                    (IV.8.39–47)

In insisting upon the ineffectiveness of these virtues in governing England, Shakespeare underlines the fact that the coincidence of political ethics, social order, and national prosperity is often accidental, always vulnerable. The model of a patriarchal and pyramidal monarchial system is shown as far less than an absolute principle of "natural" politics, as man-made rather than God-given. Throughout the Henry VI plays, such an ideology repeatedly reveals its weaknesses but is not destroyed; rather it is mutilated, somewhat as the zealots of the Reformation violated Catholic icons: the images were not simply destroyed but parts of them – the parts usually which conveyed the doctrine or meaning – defaced or disfigured, the mutilated icon then preserved in its new state of deformity. As in *3 Henry VI*, the continuity, coherence, and certainty of a totalizing worldview have been fragmented in discrete, discontinuous episodes. The character of the politically impotent but religiously orthodox king provides the equivalent stage presence of ideological values preserved but destroyed. Recent scholarly work offers us new insights into this iconoclastic urge; James R. Siemon, for example, writes:

The point of such paradoxical activity is not so much the affirmation of human continuities as a desire to reveal certain social and cultural patterns as both historically real and yet ultimately arbitrary in nature . . . . [Such] acts of desecration seem intended to force the viewer of such a [mutilated] statue into recognizing the all-important role of the human maker, into seeing the dependence of the apparently self-sufficient image on the shaping consciousness of the interpreter. Such an act insists that the image be recognized as "historical" – *made* rather than given in the nature of things.[12]

Such is the political "great chain of being": a fiction imposed upon England, historical and therefore subject to violation. Ironically, however, the effect of such iconoclasm involves the conclusion that runs opposite to the desecration of the principle once considered natural: the more political virtues and political realities are severed, the more concerned the audience becomes that they should not be. The atrocities consequent upon the ascendancy of the law of the scabbard force us to defend the civilized and to see how crucially dependent the monarchy is upon the maintenance of an ideologically consistent and forcefully administered set of coherent if "historical" fictions. The mutilated icon must be repaired, and it becomes the burden of the second tetralogy to pursue that reconstruction of kingship. It is the paradoxical ambivalence of the first to be at once subversive and conservative.

Richard of Gloucester embodies the subversively iconoclastic from his gleeful entrance with the severed head of Somerset and his advice to his father to break his oath to the murder of Henry, yet in linking Richard unambiguously with the Vice, the villain, the Machiavel, the Devil, and Judas, Shakespeare balances discord against the perception of its agent as the "devil's butcher" (V.5.75). Richard himself reinforces those identifications and sometimes introduces them: his conscious determination to act diabolically is sketched in as quickly as possible in the most public and recognizable images. Henry is thus associated with the crucified Christ, mocked by his executioners and dying with forgiveness upon his lips; Richard with those who scourged, mocked and killed Him. Perhaps even the howling dogs and some of the other images in Henry's dying speeches (V.6) would be recognized as referring to Psalm 22, a passage universally recognized as prefiguring the crucifixion and one clearly behind such paintings as Breughel's *The Crowning with Thorns*, in which one of the Roman soldiers wears a spiked dog collar.[13] The connections with the Machiavel and Sinon are Richard's own as is the final scene's aside: "so Judas kissed his master And cried 'All hail!' when as he meant all harm" (V.7.33–34).

These elements relieve the horror of the play's anarchy in the sense that through such iconoclasm the audience hears two voices. Parody must work in this manner, and the manner resembles the mutilation of images: for parody to be effective, fragments of the original must be heard. We see through the horror of York's and Henry's deaths to the Passion whose form they resemble, but we see neither as a Christ figure. The discrepancy between these agents enforces our sense of the political world disfigured by the diabolical and separated so absolutely from any spiritual realm.

Yet at the same time the fact that we know the rest of the story – Richard's future rise and fall – and that the iconoclast has been so thoroughly demonized reduces some of the anxiety which might arise from the subversiveness of the play's nihilism, of its exposure of iconicity of kingship, the inefficacy of humanist politics, and the historical fabrication of the Christianized ideology of monarchical governance. Politics in the first tetralogy is dramatized as much more problematic than the chroniclers had ever imagined; among all the melodrama and violence lies a world fractured into pieces of history, mutilated rituals, diabolical interventions, ideological fictions, and all the other destructive energies of chaos which have their own sportive elegance and artistic orderliness.

Shakespeare's success in finding maimed rites for such dances of death marks part of the achievement of 3 *Henry VI* and insures that the audience recoil from the sophisticated savagery of such atrocities, such betrayals of man's essential humanity, but it has spent its several hours in the land of cannibalism, this heart of darkness. The comedy has turned demonic, and the transformation reveals their common antagonism to the everyday world of comfortable certainties.

5

Richard III

THE ACTOR'S AUDIENCES

The theatricality of the Henry VI plays illustrates the value of analysis which at least involves if not always centers upon considerations of staging and audience response; in interpreting *Richard III* such an approach becomes unavoidable as Shakespeare concentrates upon acting, deceit, and politics as performance. Here, the audience's relationship with Richard of Gloucester and with the play itself offers almost inexhaustible complexity; the playwright entangles his spectators in their own responses, encouraging and prohibiting their seeing the action as political melodrama.

Several reminders are crucial in approaching this complexity. First, through Richard's soliloquies Shakespeare repeatedly anticipates the events of the play: Richard tells us his plots and stratagems, then we see them carried out. In the Henry VI plays, the death of Thomas Horner or the severed head of Somerset works through shock, but Richard's announcing his intentions and tactics eliminates such a theatrical effect; thus, in the play's arousing our expectations of violence, the grotesque brutality of villainy takes on a different character and engenders a more ambivalent response, especially in the first three acts where the audience is satisfied aesthetically by Richard's setting up and fulfilling dramatic expectations and is revolted morally by these same successes. Second – and related to this balance of contradictory responses – is the fact that one crucial expectation of the audience has been fixed by history; unlike the three Henry VI plays, *Richard III* has a definite moment toward which all the events must progress: the victory of Henry VII and the death of Richard. The arrangements of king, intended queen, and wily Suffolk which conclude *1 Henry VI* make good ironic sense, and the Battle of St. Albans provides satisfactory closure for Part Two. Yet these conclusions have none of the inevitability that Richard's death has;

an audience could hardly be expected to foresee them. The deaths of Prince Edward and Henry VI and the crowning of Edward IV have more obvious qualities as historical and therefore dramatic *termini*, but the audience of Part Three hardly desires the fulfilment of its expectations in the same way in which one *wills* – in a sense almost conspires with the play's intentions – the death of Richard III; on the other hard, because the audience foreknows the outcome, otherwise impermissible responses can be elicited: it can enjoy the sardonic maneuvrings of a comic Devil who will be overcome. Both of these differences change the structure of the relationships between play and audience.

The most important element in these relationships is, of course, the mediation and centrality of Richard of Gloucester's acting. Though Richard's histrionics have always been rightly described, often critical attention has stressed his successes in deception in order to explain our fascination with his villainy, while his failures to control the course of events have seemed apparent only in the last two acts. If an audience-centered analysis seems almost unavoidable with this stridently theatrical melodrama, the complicity of the audience in Richard's conspiring and his stage-managing can be exaggerated, and the distance the audience *always* feels from his machiavellian violence can be unduly minimized or even overlooked. The play's disparities and discrepancies – between what Richard says and does, thinks he has done and has done, believes in and acts upon, thinks of himself and what the audience thinks of him – compound the ironies by adding complicated dimensions of self-deception and self-division within the protagonist to the already rich and complex burdens of responding to a comic villain.

In the opening soliloquy Richard identifies himself as an actor, wearing many masks, performing many roles. *3 Henry VI* had not allowed much range for the chameleon's repertoire: a few quick allusions – sketched in the most public images at hand: the villain, the Machiavel, Sinon, Judas – tell us he is the actor-hypocrite-politician-deceiver. *Richard III* expands that range. So much is clear from the beginning: without doubt, Richard exhibits considerable histrionic talent. However, Richard has fooled many spectators (and more readers) about the extent of his cleverness. A brief sample of remarks here will help me establish a foundation for illustrating this assertion.

Charles Lamb, disappointed by Cooke's performance in 1802, wrote that Richard was not the melodramatic "monster" openly displaying his *"horns* and *claws"* but a master of "simulation," a "lofty genius," and an "experienced politician."[1] A. P. Rossiter's influential "Angel with Horns" further develops Lamb's sense of Richard's acting talents and of the play's sardonic tone and argues that Richard follows "the program set before the Prince in *Il Principe"* which demands "a lifelong, unremitting vigilance in relentless simulation and impenetrable deception." The "superhumanity of the Superman," he says, lies in his effective performance: He is an artist in evil," and the play is a "drama of consummate acting."[2] Anne Righter, concentrating upon the play's "assertions of the actor's power," describes Richard as an artist in deceit who "appears in a dazzling series of roles, all of which are completely successful. Through five long acts," she continues, "he manages to deceive virtually everyone around him, and, when the end finally comes, it is not really the result of any personal failure but the inexorable demand of Fate."[3] To these three well-known Shakespeareans might be added a host of commentaries in the same vein; though such admiration for Richard's acting is partly deserved, this firmly entrenched sense of a consummate performance is wholly misleading.

Certainly, Richard does play many roles, but at least three factors should make us hesitate to call his performance either "impenetrable" or "consummate." First, not everyone *in* the play is fooled; in fact, very few are. Second, though Richard does dominate the play, often he must share the stage, and more than once he loses control of the scene (a point I will discuss in more detail in the next section) and at other times controls it through sheer power or threats rather than through the subtleties of deception. Third, the audience's awareness that Richard is consciously playing various roles on several occasions becomes double-edged; on the one hand, we are impressed by his clever impersonations of a blunt honest counsellor or an unwilling saint or a Petrarchan lover, but we also know that the ability to *play* the role discloses a potential to *be* the thing impersonated. To the extent that he convincingly wears the mask of passionate courtier or sympathetic brother, he opens wider the disparity between what he is and what he appears to be.[4] The failure to fool all the characters within the play is matched by his failure to be the kind of men he impersonates, to have the feelings and virtues he pretends.

Who does Richard fool? Shakespeare takes care that he never fools the audience about his motives or actions, though some may be fooled about his intelligence, success, and artistry. Within the play itself, he fools Clarence into believing in his concern and his innocence while setting up Clarence's imprisonment and murder. But Clarence's subconscious reveals the truth in his bad dreams, albeit obliquely, and the Murderers subsequently undeceive him about Richard's intentions. Queen Elizabeth knows all along that Richard hates the Woodvilles and Nevilles, and he actually does his utmost to confirm her in her suspiciousness, although he also defends himself as the righteous injured party. From the beginning, she fears for young Prince Edward:

> Ah, he is young, and his minority
> Is put unto the trust of Richard Gloucester,
> A man that loves not me, nor none of you.
> (I.3.11–13)

If Elizabeth puts her only kinsmen on guard, Queen Margaret tells them again in the presence of Stanley, Hastings, and Buckingham that Richard is "the troubler of the poor world's peace" (I.3.220). Richard's own mother is not deceived about her son; she tells Clarence's children "who caused your father's death" (II.2.19) and adds:

> Ah, that Deceit should steal such gentle shape.
> And with a virtuous vizor hide deep Vice.
> (27–28)

Neither is the Duke of Buckingham deceived by Richard's acting – in fact, he provides his cues – though he temporarily trusts Richard's promise of the earldom of Hereford; finally, he knows enough of Richard's duplicity to escape (temporarily) to Brecknock while his "fearful head is on" (IV.2.122). The Scrivener clearly knows what's what as he writes out a writ of execution for an already dead man (III.6), and the citizens are not fooled by "the bastardy of Edward's children" (III.7.4) and greet Richard's performance between the Bishops with a shocked but knowing silence; even Brackenbury is suspicious of Clarence's murderers, but will not stay to "reason" what is meant by their "commission," preferring to "be guiltless" rather than be accomplice to whoever may be behind whatever they intend (I.4.93–95). King Edward is shocked by Richard's announcement of Clarence's death into a recognition of all there assembled to be reconciled as callous, ungrateful, ungracious, and self-seeking (II.1.103–135); actually, Richard almost throws his conspiracy to murder Clarence into the faces of them all as he might just as well be identifying himself:

> Some tardy cripple bore the countermand,
> That came too lag to see him buried.
>
> (90–91)

This is "nerve" not consummate acting.

Who does Richard fool? Lady Anne? Again, Richard's "nerve" bends her to his will; she is not deceived. Richard leads her from emotion to emotion, takes away her role as the grieving daughter and "wife" and assigns her a role as cruel mistress; he fascinates her, plays with her verbally and histrionically. Quite a performance it is, but deception does not adequately describe it. Part of the virtuosity of the performance lies in its transparency, in its exaggeration. Richard plies her with the Petrarchan lover's rhetoric of killing eyes and cruel beauty, then offers his sword, kneels, and "lays his breast open" (I.2.s.d.182). The revenge is offered "in terms which render it farcically irrelevant," comments Michael Neill,[5] and we might add that the farce is intended as daring and sprezzatura not as deception. No doubt, Richard plays with her, even tricks her; no doubt, his virtuosity is dazzling; no doubt, the performance is highly theatrical. But each knows the other is performing; one performer, having had the pall-bearers set down the corpse so that she can publicly, openly, ritualistically lament the dead of Henry VI and Prince Edward, has her performance interrupted by another performer, their murderer: if he feels no remorse for his deeds, she feels no real grief over their deaths. The actor and actress mirror each other. Anne calls Richard by his true names – devil, minister of hell, villain, murderer – and never takes those epithets back, but finally what we see is that Richard's amorality matters little to her: she is as weak and worthless as her opponent. Those murdered cannot serve her; Richard may. The volley of words, the exchanges of insults and compliments and then of witticisms, the histrionics of sword and ring, dramatize a battle of wills not a strategy of deception. Richard wins because he is stronger not because he is a better actor: stronger because he is more daring, has more nerve, is a man in a male-dominated world, and especially because he is a York, brother to the king, and a duke. The young widow of a Lancastrian prince has nothing on her side except her wit; even were her righteous indignation genuine, it would not count for much in this court. If Anne is deceived at all by Richard's hyperboles of love, her suspension of disbelief is willed.

To say that Richard commands the scene differs from saying that his artistry as an actor ensures his successes. The young prince wonders about the "want" of "more uncles here to welcome" his slight entourage (III.1.6), and young York, in Buckingham's words, "taunts" and "scorns" Richard "opprobriously" (153). Prince Edward hardly seems deceived by his uncle:

> *Prince.*   I fear no uncles dead.
> *Rich.*   Nor none that live, I hope?
> *Prince.*   And if they live, I hope I need not fear.
> But come, my lord: with a heavy heart,
> Thinking on them, go I unto the Tower.
> (146–50)

Similarly, Richard's trapping the unsuspecting Hastings displays "nerve" rather than histrionic talent: he simply asserts Mistress Shore's witchcraft and her lover's complicity, displaying his arm deformed from birth:

> Then be your eyes the witness of their evil.
> Look how I am bewitch'd! Behold, mine arm
> Is like a blasted sapling wither'd up.
> And this is Edward's wife, that monstrous witch,
> Consorted with that harlot, strumpet Shore,
> That by their witchcraft thus have marked me.
> (III.4.67–72)

Who is taken in by such transparent stagings? Like the murder of Clarence or the wooing of Anne, the daring accusation of Hastings would not work without control of the situation, a control which depends more upon nerve, pure power, and the moral weaknesses of the victims than upon the actor's powers. Later in Act III, Richard's and Buckingham's staged tableau of Prince Apparent flanked by Bishops does draw upon a long tradition of ceremonial and iconographic imagery to summon symbolic meanings but no one accepts them as appropriate to those managing the scenes. The silence of the Citizens underscores the Scrivener's amazement at the clarity and futility of these political charades:

> Here's a good world the while! Who is so gross
> That cannot see this palpable device?
> Yet who's so bold but says he sees it not?
> Bad is the world, and all will come to naught
> When such ill-dealing must be seen in thought.
>   (III.6.10–14)

Richard's attempt to impose an image of The Christian King bearing the burdens of monarchy upon his hunched back fails completely for both on-stage and off-stage audience.[6] It is meant to: Act III adds to the first two a sequence of manipulations which are transparent to every spectator within the play.

There exist limits to the actor's powers. To an extent, surely Richard does deceive Clarence, Anne, King Edward, and Hastings, but without the power to control the situation his acting would hardly be sufficient. As he says in the opening soliloquy: "Plots have I laid, inductions dangerous" (32). The villain as playmaker rather than as actor succeeds but partly because his little playlets are performed before captive audiences. In Thomas More's description of the Bishops Scene, the citizens see through the stage-managed public spectacle, "know right wel, that he that playeth the sowdayne is percase a sowter," and say "that these matters bee Kynges games, as it were stage playes, and for the most part plaied upon scafoldes."[7] To interrupt the proceedings would be to risk joining others on the block. Shakespeare's ironies subsume such an awareness.

I am not denying our fascination with Richard's sardonic humor, wit, and cleverness in evil; knowing the historical inevitability of Bosworth Field, an audience can afford such enjoyment: we respond to the cues he provides us, to his invitations to admire his conscious theatricality. But the spell the diabolic humorist casts is far from total; our empathetic complicity demonstrates a morally perverse capacity for enjoying the villain's murders but it accounts for only part of our response.

Much of an audience's attitude toward Richard is determined by his always playing one role for the characters within the play, another for the playhouse. For Clarence, he plays the concerned brother, for Anne the passionate courtier, for Hastings the sympathetic friend and common enemy of the Queen's upstart family; for the audience he always plays the villain. Clearly he deliberately chooses this role and openly flaunts it before us. Nevertheless, he never really inverts the normal order of moral values nor does he ignore it; he simply denies its efficaciousness and power in the world of politics. He even vigorously asserts the values of love, beauty, loyalty, and justice; he desires "friendly peace" and "all good men's love" and will "purchase" them with "duteous service" and "humility" (II.1. 60–73). So he pretends in impersonating the king's good counsellor, yet in knowing what is right and wrong – and stating normative values more clearly than any other character in the play – Richard offers his own commentary upon the immorality of his own actions. He *will* be a villain. In contrast, Anne's Edward was "that brave prince,"

> A sweeter and a lovelier gentleman,
> Fram'd in the prodigality of Nature,
> Young, valiant, wise, and, no doubt, right royal,
> The spacious world cannot again afford.
> (I.2.247–50)

He knows that he is "in So far in blood that sin will pluck on sin" (IV.2.62–63), and if he is less elaborately tortured by the scorpions of the mind than Macbeth is, both heroic villains keep the intentional pursuit of evil before their audiences. Unlike Edmund in *King Lear*, for example, Richard does not question the traditional evaluations as part of an arbitrary, man-made order of moral and social sanctions; he gives deeds and values the names moral orthodoxy would, not challenging their legitimacy but trying to exorcise them from his own mind. Because their denial entails their presence there – paradoxically, he admires his own struggle against values whose effectiveness and power he denies – the dream of the Ghosts and the soliloquy that follows should come as no surprise to an audience. Did not the restraints against murder "reside" in his mind, he could not boast so proudly of having overcome them. After this dream, he pushes away the fears it has generated, telling Norfolk, Ratcliffe, and some soldiers that

> Conscience is but a word that cowards use,

> Devis'd at first to keep the strong in awe.
> Our strong arms be our conscience, swords our law.
>
> (V.3.310–12)

Such doubletalk keeps the traditional order alive; though but words, some concept of "conscience" and "law" remains necessary for justifying his actions.

Richard deceives himself about his successes as an actor, and he deceives himself about his ability to discipline his conscience. His dream concludes with the cry "Have mercy, Jesu!" and is followed by his adding his own accusations to those of the Ghosts. He names his affliction "O coward conscience" and realizes that he cannot flee from himself:

> O no, alas, I rather hate myself
> For hateful deeds committed by myself.
> I am a villain – yet I lie, I am not!
> My conscience hath a thousand several tongues,
> And every tongue brings in a several tale,
> And every tale condemns me for a villain:
> Perjury, perjury, in the highest degree;
> Murder, stern murder, in the direst degree;
> All several sins, all us'd in each degree,
> Throng to the bar, crying all, 'Guilty, guilty!'
>
> (V.3.190–200)

With such self-knowledge, the only recourse is self-deception, the folly Richard has scorned in others.

Richard exults in the superiority of his intelligence, but he climbs to the throne more through exercise of naked force – what subtlety is involved in packing off murderers to kill Clarence and the little princes or in holding young Stanley hostage? – than through ingenious duplicity. Richard believes in the infallibility of his histrionic talents yet deceives fewer characters than he thinks he does, and he shows himself a true believer in what he had professed to deny, even in the Christ to whom he had played the antagonist. Each of these aspects of the audience's greater awareness qualifies its admiration for Richard's cleverness from the beginning.

These qualifications have seldom been thoroughly explored because many of the aspects of the dramatic structure work to obscure them. Richard's death, the unavoidable *terminus ad quem*, permits a certain amount of relaxation and enjoyment of the hero-villain, as does his identification as the Vice, the Anti-Christ, the Machiavel. But more than these structural features, the separation of Richard from the other characters profoundly alters our response to villainy. He takes us into his confidence, reveals his plots, glories in them, regards us – the off-stage spectators – as co-conspirators, and never lies to us. He acts out his chosen roles with panache and zest; among this large cast of characters he commands our admiration and attention because of his vitality and daring. Antony Hammond, the Arden editor, calls him "magnetic" and adds: "We admire his discernment of character, his address and fertility of resource, the command of his temper, his versatility, the 'alacrity' whose loss he laments on the eve of Bosworth, and his unquestioned courage and military prowess."[8] Added to these traits are his vibrant range of rhetorical styles and his salting the play with colloquial, direct, and occasionally spontaneous remarks whose incisiveness cuts through the contrasted overblown styles of address: the curses, lamentations, extended metaphors, lyrical passages, and other formal, ceremonial, and ritualized speeches.[9]

Unique to *Richard III*, the dramatic strategy sets apart one character so insistently that the action of the play has often been called a play within a play and its protagonist a puppet-master. To some extent, such comments are helpful, but again qualifications are necessary. Most of Richard's "victims" participate in their own demise; not only do they deserve the audience's scorn and whatever happens to them, but they also wilfully contribute to Richard's success. Self-interest governs everyone: Clarence naively believes his defection from the Yorkist cause will be forgotten because he wants it forgotten; Anne finds security in a profitable marriage; Edward allows his fears to displace kinship in ordering Clarence's imprisonment; even the Cardinal, who "for all this land" will not "infringe the holy privilege Of blessed sanctuary," will allow Richard to "o'er-rule my mind this once" (III.1.41–42, 57). Each actively conspires with Richard's manipulations, a conspiracy most clearly embodied in Hastings' folly of *not* playing along. Hammond comments that Hastings "is characterized particularly realistically . . . to the point that an audience can become exasperated by his wilful blindness."[10] What deceptions Richard's performances generate depend upon prior self-deceptions; Hastings, as he himself admits, is not untarnished by the violence of court politics. The

Mayor, almost comical in his deference to royalty and his credulity, readily accepts Richard's and Buckingham's word for Hastings' treason and his confession. Like Brackenbury, the Scrivener, and the Citizens in II.3 and III.7, the Mayor allows Richard's playmaking to proceed unhampered; if he might have more power than they to hinder Richard's crimes, he seems too gullible to burden with any culpability.

The moral weaknesses of his victims contribute to Richard's success and also detract from the admiration with which we regard his accomplishments. What attracts us to Richard is less his consummate skill as an actor than his audacity and his delight in villainy, an enjoyment of the intellectual sport of establishing his superiority which makes us think of Iago's motiveless malignity. To see Richard's rise to power exclusively through his own self-satisfaction with his performances is to reduce the complexities of the play's ironies and its sense of history and politics. We must look elsewhere to understand fully Richard's methods and the play's treatment of his rise and fall.

FACTION AND PROVIDENCE

When Richard steps out of the frame he has fashioned for the occasion, stands before the audience, and gives himself rave reviews for his performance, we must seriously question his evaluation of how thoroughly histrionic deception accounts for his successes. If he does "clothe" his "naked villainy With odd old ends stol'n forth of Holy Writ And seem a saint, when most I play the devil" (I.3.336–38), few are really deceived; except for Hastings, who believes he can "know" Richard's "heart" by his "face" (III.4.53), all see Richard as the ruthless, ambitious villain that he is. Nevertheless, if the on-stage characters pierce his disguises, Richard still manages – theatrically and politically – to control the stage. His acting ability only partly explains his dramatic dominance and only partly accounts for his historical success in securing the throne. The play provides us with essentially two approaches to explaining Richard's triumph, one on the level of providential ritual and the other through the making and unmaking of political factions. Occasionally these interpretations of history come into conflict, but they are not fundamentally in opposition, for the workings of Providence offer a theological explanation of *why* England had

to suffer the evils of Richard's successes, and the chess games of
faction a dramatization of *how* political power is achieved within
a political environment. And both views are deliberately hedged
with ironies that challenge any possibility of certainty about how
history works.

Setting aside the providential – at work most crucially in the
denouement – for a moment, let us look at the politics at play
in *Richard III*.[11] First, at the beginning of the play the focus has
shifted dramatically from the battlefields of *3 Henry VI* to the Court
of Edward IV, causing a rather radical change in the nature of the
world the characters inhabit. The great barons, notably Warwick
the king-maker, no longer tip the scales of power, unbalancing
rival claims to the crown and resulting in civil wars. With the
Lancastrian opponents eliminated, the Yorks enjoy the relative
peace of unchallenged sovereignty. Such is the stability described
by the opening lines:

> Now is the winter of our discontent
> Made glorious summer by this son of York;
> And all the clouds that lour'd upon our House
> In the deep bosom of the ocean buried.
> Now are our brows bound with victorious wreaths,
> Our bruised arms hung up for monuments,
> Our stern alarums chang'd to merry meetings,
> Our dreadful marches to delightful measures.
> Grim-visag'd War hath smooth'd his wrinkled front:
> And now, instead of mounting barbed steeds
> To fright the souls of fearful adversaries,
> He capers nimbly in a lady's chamber,
> To the lascivious pleasing of a lute.
>   (I.1.1–13)

This description immediately places Richard and his audience in
a Renaissance court full of lute music, dancing, amorous intrigue,
and the other "idle pleasures" (31) of a courtier's life. Though the
wars in the Low Countries and the troubles with Spain could
not be dismissed from Elizabeth's policy-making, they were not
to be dwelled on, and her Court, like those on the Continent,
stressed the accomplishments of civilized entertainment. Richard
finds himself within what to him are the confining expectations of

sixteenth-century "courtesy" and cannot endure the repression of his military instincts.

He would not have to. The elegant splendor at court offered equally violent diversions. Elizabeth's court politics featured the sport of faction, clientage, and patronage to engage the ambitiousness of the monarch's servants.[12] *Richard III* mirrors but does not directly reflect the ideological environment of the Elizabethan jockeying for power and prestige. Although the play begins with everyone at court – except Richard, of course – moderately satisfied that the hostilities between the Yorks and the Lancasters have ended, the cessation of violence is only apparent, because there are fears and factions at Edward's court. Richard can play upon his brother's fears that Clarence will remain an untrustworthy ally, brother, and counsellor; he has, after all, betrayed the Yorkist cause once in defecting to Warwick. If in the first scene Richard boasts about the plotting that will lead to Clarence's death, later he blames the Queen's party – the Woodvilles and Nevilles – for urging King Edward to execute him. The two sources of animosity toward Clarence complement rather than contradict each other, as Richard can take advantage of a faction-ridden court to trigger fears and suspicions. The strategy here has a two-pronged effect: Richard will eliminate his older brother and therefore another relative between himself and the throne and will also weaken the king's loyal friends and everyone's trust in the Woodvilles.[13]

Under Edward, many of the nobility – those left after the bloodiness of the Wars of the Roses – have been drawing the lines: the king's family versus the Queen's. Richard must destroy both and refashion an alliance with himself as the center; he cannot simply murder his way to the crown: he must smile and be a villain. With Clarence out the way, Edward has no intimate family members (except Richard) to support him. The faction at court which revolves around Queen Elizabeth, Lady Grey, has gained considerable power. Anthony Woodville, Earl Rivers, her brother, and Lord Grey and the Marquess of Dorset, her sons, are assumed to be constantly present at court, influencing Edward's decisions. Presumably, these Woodvilles can count upon Sir Thomas Vaughan and a number of other lords – especially the Nevilles, who sided with the Lancasters, their relatives by marriage, during the late wars – to support them. In the middle are unaligned noblemen, and these are the potentially loyal followers of Richard's inchoate faction. Hastings and Buckingham represent those influential courtiers angry about Edward's foolish marriage to Lady Grey, a marriage of no dynastic nor national value which has resulted in the advancement of the undeserving queen's family to the rank of royal gentlemen and their consequent siphoning off of preferments, rewards, and prestige from the worthy lords they know they are. Edward, they know, could have made a good match but instead has peopled his court with these upstart families. Richard shrewdly plays upon their snobbery and understandable aggravation, making the Queen's family into newly dressed fops, ducking with "French nods and apish courtesy" (I.3.49), "silken, sly, insinuating Jacks," these pretenders to aristocracy (53). Richard openly challenges the Woodville party, accusing them of both Clarence's death and Hastings' imprisonment, playing upon the lack of credibility in a court split by faction and intrigue and appealing to the hatred of the old royal blood for the "new royalty." Though he may exaggerate or twist the truth, Richard does not have to use deceit to convince others of the venality of the Queen's faction; he tells his brother that they have turned the court into a fearful, inverted world in which the truly noble have no place:

> *Rich.* Why, this it is, when men are rul'd by women:
> Tis not the King that sends you to the Tower;
> My Lady Grey, his wife, Clarence, 'tis she
> That tempers him to this extremity.
> Was it not she, and that good man of worship,
> Anthony Woodeville, her brother there,
> That made him send Lord Hastings to the Tower,
> From whence this present day he is deliver'd?
> We are not safe, Clarence, we are not safe!
> *Clar.* By heaven, I think there is no man secure,
> But Queen's kindred, and night-walking heralds
> That trudge between the King and Mistress Shore.
> (I.1.62–73)

The response confirms the plausibility of Richard's interpretation and also re-emphasizes the amorous pleasures of their brother and suggests his debaucheries in which the queen's sons were thought by some of Shakespeare's sources to be participants. Richard argues that Elizabeth and Mistress Shore have displaced Edward's brothers as his royal council, as "mighty gossips in our monarchy" (83). If the "our" already suggests to the audience Richard's proprietary expectations about the throne, to Clarence it must recall the three suns in one, the Yorkist monarchy. Later, Richard uses the term "faction" directly and negatively in casting himself as the innocent, injured party (I.3.57) and allies his disgrace to the "nobility Held in contempt" (79–80) by the queen's family. He reminds the Woodvilles (and the audience) that the basis for his animosity is genuine: Elizabeth, her first husband, Lord Grey, and her brother, Lord Rivers, had been "factious for the House of Lancaster" and fought against the Yorks at St. Albans (127–30).

Against this background Richard's maneuvrings take on a less melodramatic coloring and begin to suggest an understanding of how power might work within a monarchy not totally unlike Shakespeare's own. The Cecils – Lord Burghley and his son William – were an upstart family: though not Elizabeth I's family, they began humbly and in the 1590s controlled policy and preferments at her Court, frustrating the ambitions of the old royal blood, particularly the demands for service and office made by Robert Devereux, the Earl of Essex, for himself and for other aristocratic courtiers. The recalcitrance of the Cecils, nearly all-powerful with Elizabeth in her last years, more than any other factor prompted Essex's rebellion, a last attempt to oust them from power. If, at the time *Richard III* was written, the faction-fighting of the Cecil/Essex parties was most prominent, Elizabethans, especially the nobility, had long been concerned with the power of factions at the monarch's court. In the *Arcadia* Sir Philip Sidney had described the confusion attendant upon the supposed death of King Basilius: the state became "altogether like a falling steeple: the parts whereof . . . were well but the whole mass ruinous . . . the great men looking to make themselves strong by factions; the gentlemen, some bending to them, some standing upon themselves, some desirous to overthrow those few they thought were over them."[14] There are no direct equivalents to contemporary politics in *Richard III*, but the play rather dramatically stages the process described by Sidney and later by Francis Bacon in his *Essays* (circulating in the 1590s before their first printing in 1597) and acted out weekly at Elizabeth I's court.[15]

Richard of Gloucester understands that process well. He convinces "the new-deliver'd Hastings" (I.1.121) that the Queen's faction has sent him to the Tower; he complains on behalf of the old royal blood (I.3.77–81) and makes himself into the champion

of the true nobility. Perhaps Buckingham's animosity toward the queen's party has a similar origin: we do not know from the play exactly why he adheres to Richard's plotting, but Francis Bacon's generalization may apply to him as well: "Factious followers . . . Follow not vpon Affection to him with whom they raunge Themselues, but vpon Discontentment Conceiued against some Other."[16] So the courtier and follower of Essex wrote in the 1590s after failing in his pursuit of the high office of Attorney-General, a failure which resulted from complex ambiguities at Elizabeth's court and one which might be studied with the other failures, miscalculations, ironic successes, and confusions of Sidney, Ralegh, Donne, Spenser, and doubtless hundreds of other courtiers whose expectations of advancement went unfulfilled. In any case, in the farce of King Edward's attempt to reconcile all parties at court, Buckingham is identified with Hastings as having been "factious" against the Woodvilles, and after Edward's death it is Buckingham who shrewdly contributes to Richard's plotting against the Queen's kindred:

> *Buck.*   My lord, whoever journeys to the Prince,
> For God's sake let not us two stay at home:
> For by the way I'll sort occasion,
> An index to the story we late talk'd of,
> To part the Queen's proud kindred from the Prince.
>   *Rich.*   My other self, my counsel's consistory,
> My oracle, my propher, my dear cousin:
> I, as a child, will go by thy direction.
>   (II.2.146–53)

Although named one of the "many simple gulls" (I.3.328) that Richard will gather to his side by exaggerating the Woodvilles' treachery to Edward, Buckingham certainly understands th importance of faction as well as Richard.

One of Richard's first plots involves marrying Anne Nevil' youngest daughter of the last remnant of the family connecti back to John of Gaunt and Edward III, thus consolidating his po and covering the Yorkist flank; later, in pursuing his niece, Qu Elizabeth's and Edward's daughter, he wishes to secure or at ' pre-empt the power of the Woodvilles. His blackmailing Sta dramatizes a desperate effort to maintain his ascendancy amor old nobility, even after he has executed Hastings and Buckin⸴

and others have abandoned him. Ironically, the triumph of Henry VII does not re-unite the ancient families of York and Lancaster but ushers in the control of the English throne by the union of two "new and rising" ones: the Woodvilles and Tudors. And Shakespeare makes that point very clearly.

Equally familiar to some of the Elizabethan audience should have been some of Richard's methods. Aligned with Richard's faction are the ambitious noblemen: Sir William Catesby, Sir Richard Ratcliffe, Lord Lovell, and Sir James Tyrrell. Their talents range from sounding out the hesitant Hastings to murdering the young princes. Richard's emphasis upon a loyal intelligence service suggests corresponding efforts at surveillance during the 1590s, efforts which the absence of an effective police force may have made necessary but which angered many of those who felt themselves under scrutiny. Though perhaps *Hamlet* provides a clearer and more powerful staging of the watchers at court, Catesby embodies the style of entrapment essential to the intrigues of faction-fighting and sometimes state government; similar measures were tried with the imprisoned Ben Jonson in an attempt to get him to incriminate himself.[17] Hastings is victimized by his own loyalty to Edward V, thus dramatizing not so much the folly of trusting the wrong man but the rashness of trying to stand independently of faction. The scene in which he meets first a pursuivant and then a priest has been read as an iconographic tableau whose dramaturgy originated in the mystery and morality plays: the sinful man caught between the agents of authority, secular and spiritual.[18] That description accurately captures the foolishness of the politician who believes he can limit his criminality and sinfulness and control his fortunes with man and God. But the common association of pursuivants, officers who had the power to serve warrants, with surveillance, spying, and arbitrary arrests links Hastings' fate to Richard's methods in forcing the old nobility to cast their loyalty to one party or the other. John Donne writes, for example, of the arrogance of those who spied out Roman Catholics in the 1590s; even the holiest of men might be angered

> To see a Pursivant come in, and call
> All his cloathes, Copes; Bookes, Primers; and all
> His Plate, Challices; and mistake them away,
> And ask a fee for comming . . .
>
> ("Satire V")[19]

Noting the presence of the pursuivant, Shakespeare's audience might have assumed that Richard was having Hastings watched; in any case, the arbitrary labelling of Hastings' conspiracy against the Lord Protector reveals itself in the patently absurd accusation of witchcraft, a "mistake" as outrageous as the one Donne describes. Along with Richard's pretense of humility, ensconced between the bishops, and with his dissembling opposition to Edward's "evil diet" which has "over-much consum'd his royal person" (I.1.139–40), we see and see through the "mock-Puritan" mask the deformed brother, unfit for amorous pleasures of the time, chooses to wear. Greenblatt's association of power and sexuality offers provocative generalizations:

> Power . . . is not only the ability to levy taxes or raise and army but the ability to enforce submission, manifested in those signs of secular worship – bowing, kneeling, kissing of rings – that European rulers increasingly insist upon. If these signs always have an air of fiction about them – and indeed in England they beome increasingly fantastic until they reach the aesthetic mania of the court of Charles I – so much the better, because, as we have argued, one of the highest achievements of power is to impose fictions upon the world and one of its supreme pleasures is to enforce the acceptance of fictions that are known to be fictions.[20]

If Richard makes the nobility, the commons, and minor functionaries (such as Brackenbury and the Scrivener) acknowledge his sovereignty, and if he does so at the expense of credibility, he succeeds well enough at forging a powerful faction that persuading his subjects to *believe* his fictions becomes unnecessary. Moreover, the sexuality of such exercises of power is almost always evoked implicitly as one of the most compelling pleasures of his triumphs.

Yet the matter becomes more complex with Richard's coronation. Though the most theatrical of roles, that of the king seems beyond his talents. Richard is absolutely unable to carry out the impersonation of Kingship and forfeits the kingdom partly because he cannot manage the symbolism of the throne.[21] He is finally "himself alone," as he himself insists upon dramatizing in his first scene of pomp and ceremony: "Stand all apart!" (IV.2.1). Having so thoroughly based his sense of his own identity upon the disparity of man and role, face and mask, Richard cannot simply unite them and become the

king, however clearly he believes he understands the conventions
of royal theatricality. His first act from the throne is to question
Buckingham's loyalty by attempting to draw him into the murder
of the princes, and when he fails to command immediate assent, he
is disconcerted. As we see him in this crucial scene act and react,
the play denies him any regality by presenting his insecurities
about the princes, Buckingham, the strength of the faction he has
formed by marrying Anne, Stanley, and finally Richmond. As he
exits after refusing Buckingham the earldom he had promised, he
must leave the throne empty on an empty stage, a visual moment in
the theatergoer's experience which sums up the fictionality of this
stage of politics by separating the office from its symbols. In the
next moment Tyrrel re-enters upon the empty stage for his lengthy
and remorseful soliloquy: "The tyrannous and bloody act is done"
(IV.3.1ff.). Richard must, therefore, re-enter his own throne-room
to greet the murderer who now alone occupies it and on the same
stage level. Later, when Ratcliffe enters with bad news from the
battlefront, Richard himself underscores the lack of ceremony at his
court by remarking that he "com'st in so bluntly" (45).

Throughout the last two acts, Shakespeare repeatedly stages
images of Richard's failure to play the king, manage the theatrical
symbols of royalty, and command the powers which belong to
sovereignty. But the inability to play the role does not alone account
for Richard's doom; during these last two acts Richmond attracts
those of the old nobility to his side, adding the powers of the
remaining Woodville son, Dorset, and securing a marriage to Queen
Elizabeth's daughter. If Richard has gained the throne by mounting
a powerful faction, now he has lost that advantage to Richmond,
as progressively more noblemen join his party: Morton, Bishop of
Ely, and Buckingham (IV.3.46–49), Dorset, Sir Edward Courtney,
the Bishop of Exeter, the Guilfords, Sir Thomas Lovel (IV.4.467,
500, 503, 518), and the long list detailed by Sir Christopher Urswick
at Stanley's request(V.5.12–15): the role call of Herbert, Talbot,
Stanley, Oxford, Pembroke, Blunt, and Rice ap Thomas sounds
the names of the old nobility Richard had thought to marshall to
his side. He who lives by faction dies by faction.

Richard III stages a very clear explanation of how history works
through the creation, dissolution, and re-creation of factions, an
understanding which seems to take precedence over the public
management of royal theatricality and which accounts for the
political rise and fall of the tyrant-villain in completely human

terms. As such this dramatization seriously questions the sacra-
mental and ideological emphasis upon the divinity of kingship
and the providential appointment of the first Tudor as national
savior, but it does not totally discredit that reading of history. By
offering an alternative sense of how politics might have worked, the
play provides us with compelling evidence that the determinants
affecting the outcome of historical events can be understood at a
completely cultural level.

The approach to the politics of *Richard III* I have just outlined
is usually overlooked largely because of the play's presentation of
the providential ordering of history. The chronicle sources provided
Shakespeare with material for both approaches but emphasized
more strongly the providential ritual of intervention by a benevolent divinity shaping England's history through a process of sin
and expiation. *Richard III* does not accept this view uncritically,
neither does it present the providential historians' hindsight as
incompatible with the faction-fighting of the drama's present tense.
The play encircles this view with irony, primarily by detaching it
from any credible authority, creating distortions of it which often
appear parodies because of the self-serving characters who voice
their beliefs in providence. Yet even such ambivalence cannot
destroy the providential view, for the anchor slipped and the ship
of certainty carried along by the tempest of irony, Providence once
again becomes inscrutable, partly as a result of the unauthoritative
voices of characters with radically limited perspectives who speak
as her prophets and interpreters.

Queen Margaret repeatedly urges the providential theory of
history upon both on-stage and off-stage audience. Though not
alone in her belief in God's intervention in man's history, from
her first appearance (I.3.) to her last (IV.4) she is constantly calling
upon the retributive justice of a God who punishes evil deeds.
She curses her enemies and prophesies that divine vengeance will
overcome their present state of comfort, and almost every one of
her prophesies is fulfilled. The mechanism of just rewards attains
a powerful and fierce rhetoric through her long, stylized, bitter
recriminations, and because those cursed do fall in the course of
the play, she seems at first thought to be in tune with the higher
power which orders human affairs.

What are we to make of Shakespeare's deliberate repetition
and stress upon this highly symmetrical pattern? In performance,
because of its length, second only to *Hamlet*, *Richard III* is usually

severely cut, and Margaret's role is often the first to go. In a way, this omission seems logical; after all, the historical Margaret had left England for France in 1475 and had died in 1482, before the death of Edward IV. What is a Lancaster doing in a York court? However, her presence precisely dramatizes Shakespeare's deviation from the chroniclers' easy acceptance of the Tudor myth. Why should the playwright intentionally create a major part which was historically indefensible and dramatically illogical? If Margaret clearly enunciates the righteous orthodoxy that all sinners must meet their just rewards, she does so in the most warped and hysterical manner. Through Margaret, the play constantly parodies providential "justice": for her, all Yorks become sinners in the hands of an angry God bent upon the destruction of all the Lancasters' enemies. Although they deserve hellfire, can we imagine a God who will respond to this bitter old woman's cries for vengeance? That her curses are actually fulfilled works against the providential view; the feeling and tone – cruel, bloody, almost as Satanic as Richard's – call for a mechanical wrath. As long as Margaret remains its constant stage presence and embodiment, the ironies militate against our regarding the providential interpretation of events without ambivalence. If others share her view, that merely extends the questioning ironies. Moody Prior comments that "The belief of these characters in a divine justice is entirely self-serving, without an ethical base . . . . for these people, living in a frightful and disordered world, belief in the operation of a divine retributive justice provides a sense of moral order . . . but it keeps alive the urge for private vengeance and relieves them of a feeling of responsibility for wrongs suffered by others."[22] For Margaret the greater irony is that she deserves eternal condemnation for the crimes she has committed and must be punished by the same principles of retributive fulfilment. Her own ritualized mockery of the Crucifixion in the parodic murder of York surpasses anything Richard (Anti-Christ and Devil) does or even contemplates. Margaret would have God as easily and as brutally execute her orders as did Clifford in *3 Henry VI*.

The inclusion of Margaret, last remnant of the Lancastrian glory, does not really advance the plot, nor do Clarence's children in II.2 or the little princes in II.4 and III.1. They take the stage to present the inadequacies of the providential view. Margaret's appropriation of a vengeful God parodies it; the princes show the audience an innocence which must suffer and die before Richard's evil. Satisfying in its neatness and clarity, the union of the houses of York and Lancaster through Richmond can only come about through the destruction of innocence. Is this how Providence works? Can one entertain the concept of a God who fulfils Margaret's curses or who advances His schemes for the Tudor hegemony through the deaths of young Edward and York? What Shakespeare has accomplished is not the discrediting of the providential ritual of Edward Hall and the other chroniclers, but by displacing this view on to a character who can by no means claim any authority, he makes us question the reductiveness of any simplistic accounting procedure. In addition, Margaret's view keeps before the audience the transhuman forces which make human plots for power and kingdom precarious enterprises at best; that most of her "prophesies" are fulfilled more than incidentally underlines this warning and adds to the ironies of hoist-on-their-own-petards over-reaching. In Nicholas Brooke's succinct summary: Shakespeare's "irony in fact works both ways: if it mocks the human, it also questions the divine."[23] But that irony itself is problematized by further ironies, as the fifth-act triumph of Richmond re-instates the providential with the authority of history's truth and the unambivalent characterization of England's salvific champion. The definite invitation to interpret Richard as God's Scourge complements this authority with the supporting irony of the Satanic impersonator's evil turned to good. Moreover, one grand irony of Richmond's ascendancy reflects upon Margaret's myopia: this final event, which accords so well with her schemes of vengeance, is the most prominent prophesy she has failed to make, although her ineffectual husband had foreseen it. If the play's conclusion suggests we grant this interpretation of history priority, the audience, however pleased that this terrible stretch of its own anarchic past has come to an end, also knows that history allowed no alternative conclusion. The ironies, distortions, and parodies of the first four acts are silenced with the death of the villain who has absorbed and come to embody all the evils plaguing England.

Were the audience simply to rejoice with Henry VII in his defeat of "God's enemy" and praise Divine Providence for its wisdom in restoring the nation to peace, prosperity, and moral government, the politics of *Richard III* could be confined to the conservative mythologizing of the Tudor myth. But central to the play's treatment of the history of the villain-king is its insistence upon the paradox that Richard himself and not God has cast himself in the role of the Vice, Machiavel, Devil, Anti-Christ, tyrant, and villain. Richard assigns himself the part as God's enemy and imposes that dramatic design upon history; that God need not really intervene while such a playmaker invents "plots dangerous" for himself provides additional and double-sided ironies which question the divine and mock the human. More than a few critics have been repelled by the apparent paradox of "the Cosmic Ironist" employing an avenging "angel with horns" to do the work of Providence,[24] but what seems more obvious is the play's ambivalence about the intervention of the all-knowing deity: the play provides us with completely satisfying dramatic explanations for every event on the human level, while offering us plenty of structural, poetic, and symbolic associations for arriving at an interpretation of the same affairs of men at a level of providential ritual. Even for Richard, the two views do not conflict, for he does not himself deny the existence nor power of God, nor does he really hold fundamentally unorthodox moral views. Only because he is a man with a conscience, can he enjoy the delights of transgressing the limits of morality and political humanism; proving himself a villain shall be his major joy in life, he announces in his opening speech, a soliloquy from which the ambition for the throne is totally absent. It is the play's irony that Richard chooses evil, and although Providence may elect to accomplish good through evil and although it is history and not fiction that is being dramatized, the play's irony cannot be so readily and absolutely transferred to the deity. The chroniclers' "reading" of the reign of the monstrous Gloucester is neither discredited not validated; it becomes an interpretation which must compete for our attention and assent.

6

King John

"There are no heroes, only victims," says one of the characters in Friedrich Durrenmatt's *König Johan: Nach Shakespeare*.[1] Though an exaggeration if applied to Shakespeare's *King John*, this statement succinctly describes the early histories: the plays of the first tetralogy and *John* sardonically deflate the heroics of politics and attain some of their most effective theatrical moments by mocking the rhetoric and ceremony of history.[2]

Plays without heroes cause both literary critics and theater directors trouble. The problems with *King John* have often been attributed to the absence of a central character, and though this want of a hero to dominate the entire play contributes to our interpretive difficulties, there are other structural peculiarities also. In the study, of course, we may find that England is the hero of the histories, suffering the tragedy of misrule, civil war, and international politics and enjoying the momentary triumphs of peace, empire, and prosperity. Once a very popular play, *John* ends with a rousing note of nationalism:

> Now these her princes are come home again
> Come the three corners of the world in arms
> And we shall mock them! Nought shall make us rue
> If England to itself do rest but true!
> (V.7.115–18)

George Bernard Shaw, reviewing Beerbohm Tree's 1899 production, found that this last speech by the Bastard "rings out those words in which the poetry of patriotism finds the noblest expression it can find."[3] If Shaw's experience in the theater seems to confirm England as hero in *John*, this Armada idiom is skewed by the

123

ironic underminings of John's criminality, the Barons' treachery, the Bastard's naval incompetence, and the final stage image of the boy Henry as king. The patriotic ring is heard only after the discords of a very thoroughgoing parody of nationalism. This ambivalence Shakespeare's play explores effectively in many scenes, less successfully in others.

This ambivalence is reflected in both the dramatic structure and the characters. The threat to John's throne in Chatillon's defiance opens the play but is completely dissolved with the diplomatic compromise of Lewis's marriage to Blanche; at the end of Act II the play's initial plot is over. Only with the entrance of Pandulph (III.1.61) does the play regain a plot of any kind. Furthermore, these two structural issues are related, because with the temporary closure of the marriage, it looks as if John has solved his problem – Arthur may be the "true king" but without the French he and Constance have no power – and has acted decisively, albeit expediently rather than heroically and honorably. He, therefore, presents an illusion of strength. Even with the challenge of Pandulph, John vigorously vows to "allay" his "rage" with "The blood, and dearest-valued blood, of France" (III.1.269). To this point, John appears kingly enough: he has led troops to France, besieged a city, and forced a treaty from King Philip by trading only Blanche of Castile and a dowry of five provinces for peace. All appearances suggest that John has gained the upper hand, shrewdly disarming his opponents with swift military action and expedient diplomatic compromise. Yet the next appearance of John provides the emotional turning point in the play, as Johns solicits Hubert to kill Arthur (III.2).[4]

By examining this first movement of the play, we can see in what sense the titular character is the central figure in *King John*. In the first two acts, John acts quickly to invade France, Fortune smiles on John, and the alliance of Constance, Arthur, and Philip is broken by the marriage, thus bringing the first plot to an end. These coincidences do not occur accidentally, for the central issue revolves around the question of legitimacy versus "right," of political power and its sources. At the very beginning of Act I, disregarding historical fact, Shakespeare removes any pretense of legitimacy from King John, establishing him clearly as a usurper and one constantly conscious of this status (I.1.40–41). That the matter of the legitimacy of the ruler involves more than merely primogeniture and hereditary succession is dramatized by several variations on the theme of law versus might: by the Falconbridges' dispute; by Constance's and Arthur's appeal to France (the traditional enemy) and Austria (the slayer of Richard I, Arthur's uncle); and by Blanche's marriage to Lewis. Each of these three scenes portrays the making of a deal which will gain the parties an advantage but at the expense of either common human values or what is "right" in an absolute sense. Philip Falconbridge trades legitimacy and inheritance for a knighthood and the honor of being Richard Coeur-de-Lion's bastard. Constance bargains an alliance at the cost of an English-French war. Lewis finds that he can love Blanche for five provinces. Certainly, John is not alone in attempting to determine the price at which his adversaries will "sell out" their honor or principle.[5]

In these first two acts, Shakespeare establishes the division of right and might: no one has both. Arthur, the "true king," can muster no power without European allies; John maintains the throne by "strong possession" (I.1.39–40). To make the issue more problematic, Arthur's royalty hardly extends beyond his being Geoffrey's son: "I would that I were laid low in my grave," he says; "I am not worth this coil that's made for me" (II.1. 164–65). The Falconbridge dispute underlines this division: the illegitimate Philip is found "perfect Richard" the Lionhearted (I.1.90). The repetition of "right" or "rights" six times in the first forty lines of the play further emphasizes the theme.

Behind this question of right versus might lies the larger question of power. Without the traditional source of power in the legitimate hereditary succession of the crown, John must seek other sources of power. "Strong possession," the major source of power, must be buttressed by the fierce rhetoric of masculine kingliness, the quick action of military invasion, the value of land (the five provinces), family bloodline (Blanche), loyalty to the crown, knighthood, and in the later acts promises of "advantage" to Hubert (III.2.32) and of at least ceremonial yielding to the Pope (V.1). Moreover, actions which would draw praise in more normal circumstances become ambivalent where initiated by John. He defends England against foreign powers, but he himself has forced Constance into a French alliance through his usurpation. He rebukes the Pope's emissary and Rome's "usurp'd authority" (III.1.86) in ordering an English king, but in assuming the "great supremacy" of the Church of England John is also establishing a source of funds for his wars, an excuse to "shake the bags / Of hoarding abbots" (III.2.17–18).

The first two acts further stress that these sources of power depend upon the military or moral weakness of John's opponents or upon their willingness to bargain. Because the balance of military strength will change, because the number of bargains is finite, because promises will not be kept, power based upon these sources – rather than upon the more traditional inheritance of the crown – is temporary. In short, John's success in the first two acts depends upon Fortune. Constance iterates this theme as another one of division; addressing Arthur, she says:

> Nature and fortune join'd to make thee great:
> Of nature's gifts thou mayst with lilies boast
> And with the half-blown rose. But fortune, O,
> She is corrupted, chang'd and won from thee;
> Sh' adulterates hourly with thine uncle John
> And with her golden hand hath pluck'd on France
> To tread down fair respect of sovereignty,
> And made his majesty the bawd to theirs.
> France is a bawd to fortune and King John,
> That strumpet fortune, that usurping John!
>   (II.2.52–61)

The separation of qualities or factors which belong together forms the basis for these first two acts – and for failure. Right without might, royalty without legitimacy, nature without fortune – and all these vice versa – can stand alone only temporarily.

The role of Fortune is underscored through her impeding Chatillon's return with "adverse winds" (II.1.57) and her providing John with good ones, so good that the French several times declare their astonishment at John's speedy arrival (II.1.79 and 233). Later, Fortune turns against John, hastening the French invasion (IV.2.113–15) and "devouring" the English forces by the "unexpected flood" of the tides in the Lincoln Washes (V.6.39–41 and V.7.61–65). Fortune cannot be controlled; John is no Atropos:

> K. John   Why do you bend such solemn brows on me?
> Think you I bear the shears of destiny?
> Have I commandment on the pulse of life?
>   Salis.   It is apparent foul-play; and 'tis shame
> That greatness should so grossly offer it:
> So thrive it in your game! and so, farewell.
>   (IV.2.90–95)

The irony here, of course, is that John has tried to assume the role, urging Hubert to murder Arthur, but has failed. But more than that, by linking Fortune, play, and game, this exchange points up the game of politics which men may play but whose outcome Fortune determines. Having, as he believes, a handful of trumps, Lewis repeats these associations when at Pandulph's request he refuses to back away from the invasion:

> Have I not here the best cards for the game
> To win this easy match play'd for a crown?
> (V.2.105–6)

Images of chess (II.1.122–23 and V.2.141) also emphasize the gamesmanship of politics. Games of skill and strategy like cards and chess also involve the element of chance, and in the larger game of politics one cannot rely upon the unpredictable turns of strumpet Fortune in determining the behavior of men and the weather at sea.

Several conclusions follow from this analysis. The dramatic structure of *King John* owes much to the older patterns of "the fall of princes" and "the Wheel of Fortune" paradigms for tragic action. Certainly *John* offers no simple, negative "mirror for magistrates," but instead shows how problematic English history is. Second, *John* stands as an interesting experiment among the early history plays in its contrast with the first tetralogy's use of Providence as the pervasive (albeit ambivalent) image of supernatural influence upon history. Third, as with the associations of metaphors of game, play, and fortune, so too do the play's characters reinforce the audience's perception of John's centrality in the dramatic structure. The Bastard's asides, interruptions, suggestions, and soliloquies function primarily to define the nature of the play's world of expedient politics and only secondarily to reveal his character. The soliloquies, "A foot of honour" (I.1.182–219) and "Mad world, mad kings" (II.1.561–95), mock the world of deceit and commodity with satire which must be considered essentially choric.

The inevitable conclusion must be that *King John*'s dramatic structure is more unified and logical than we are likely to notice in the study. From Chatillon's entrance to John's death – and even beyond in the accession of the boy king Henry III, who was known, as Walter Pater points out, by Shakespeare's audience as a "picturesque though useless king"[6] – the throne of England is beset by threats; one after another, alliances are formed against

John. Even the temporary peace at the end of Act II (and before Pandulph's first appearance) promotes a theatrically effective illusion of problems solved, a hiatus in the structure of challenges to be met, opponents to be bought off or otherwise disposed of. The extensive contrasts and parallels of John's and Lewis's rises and falls, John's domination by and freedom from Eleanor and Philip, his contemplated murders of Arthur and the English nobles, the betrayals of Hubert and Melun, John's submissions to Pandulph, the English loss of its forces at sea – all these highlight the risks of politics and the turning Wheel of Fortune. However ill-considered, the rapid changes in allegiance and alliance form a logic of plot which terrifies the audience with the radical instabilities of the political world.

Berners Jackson's review of the *King John* directed by Peter Dews at Stratford, Ontario, in 1974 illustrates that such a logic of plot can be staged persuasively:

> What Dews's production made clear beyond doubt was the essence of the play's action lies in that besetting [of King John], in the relentless construction of a net of people and events around the figure of the increasingly inept king. When the play focuses in that way on the destruction of the unprincipled and vacillating monarch, its scarifying comment on political man is sharpened and at the same time tempered with compassion.[7]

As John's stratagems in maintaining power become more desperate, culminating in his request that Hubert murder Arthur, his fortunes change. Even John himself knows not only that his luck is running out but also that he can gain no sure source of power through eliminating the rightful heir. Shakespeare leaves it unclear whether he repents his criminal intention or its failure to secure his position:

> K. John   They burn in indignation . . . I repent:
> There is no sure foundation set on blood,
> No certain life achiev'd by others' death.
>   (IV.2.103–5)

The politics of expediency leads inevitably and relentlessly to more risky and more cruel actions, as the series of opposing alliances and unfortunate outcomes forces John to react with one new tactic after another. To be sure, John's character deteriorates from the middle to the end of the play, but his downfall cannot evoke merely cheers from an audience. Just as the social atmosphere of violent feuding in *Romeo and Juliet* generates a world in which accidents can be expected to happen, in *King John* the usurper's bargains, machinations, and violence produce a world in which Fortune can be expected to change favor.

John finally becomes as pitiful as he has been villainous. He finds no moment for introspection, and he finally gives up, a defeated monarch, before he is poisoned at Swinstead. C. Cowden Clarke describes a performance by Charles Macready which captured some of John's fall:

> They who fortunately witnessed the performance [in 1842] will not forget the manner in which Mr. Macready impersonated the King, and the artistical way in which he demonstrated the unhappiness of wickedness throughout; the gradual and constant declension of his spirit, its tide being always at the ebb; his small amount of confidence, his suggested consciousness of meanness, guilt, and the loss of all respect; his bearing latterly as that of a man who felt that indignant eyes were flashing on him, and his gait as if surrounded by pitfalls; in short, the general substratum of wretchedness which pervades the whole character, and yet is only known and felt, not blazoned; all this unprotruded demeanor . . . greatly surpassed in merit the conception even of his dying scene, terrifically real as that was.[8]

No doubt, King John can never play as a great tragic role, yet some sense of his doomed struggle to face out the "borrowed majesty" that comes with usurpation should accompany his search for sources of power to provide the needed grounds of authority and stability. Without the moral order and symbolism of legitimate succession, John's reign can only be criminal. Henry IV will face the same problem but handle it in more sophisticated ways.

To portray a John erratic, childish, jittery, and manic confuses the issues the play presents.[9] For all his failings, John does command the loyalty of Hubert and the Bastard, who display no simple-minded patriotism but a noble and not simply pragmatic allegiance to their king. The Bastard, for example, knows that history is in the making and that all are on stage; at the siege of Angiers, he attempts to move beyond the stalemate:

> By heaven, these scroyles of Angiers flout you, kings,

> And stand securely on their battlements,
> As in a theatre, whence they gape and point
> At your industrious scenes and acts of death.
>
> (II.1.373–76)

The theater of politics or the game of politics: John must play – or withdraw, as he ultimately does. When the Bastard assumes the royal rhetoric, the play metaphors reappear:

> Now hear our English king,
> For thus his royalty doth speak in me:
> He is prepared, and reason too he should –
> This apish and unmannerly approach,
> This harness'd masque and unadvised revel . . . .
>
> (V.2.128–32)

However consious of the artifice and folly, the actors must play out this stage dance in armor that is war.

This consciousness of the absurdity of politics, of the necessity of rhetoric, role-playing, and gamesmanship, provides a connection between John and the Bastard seldom observed. If Macready was right to suggest in John a pervasive "consciousness" of "the unhappiness of wickedness," the inner life of John is given some illumination. Samuel Johnson's note discusses these possibilities quite fully:

> A man engaged in wickedness would keep the profit to himself, and transfer the guilt to his accomplice. These reproaches, vented against Hubert, are not the words of art or policy, but the eruptions of a mind swelling with consciousness of a crime, and desirous of discharging its misery on another. This account of the timidity of guilt is drawn *ab ipsis recessibus mentis*, from the intimate knowledge of mankind, paricularly that line in which he says, that *to have bid him tell his tale* in *express words*, would have struck him dumb: nothing is more certain than that bad men use all the arts of fallacy upon themselves, palliate their actions to their own minds by gentle terms, and hide themselves from their own detection in ambiguities and subterfuges.[10]

In acting and reacting constantly, John has been allowed little time for introspection; indeed, perhaps Johnson's "eruptions" does seem appropriate. Nevertheless, his only moment of apparent remorse is mixed with his attempts to shift all the blame for Arthur's murder onto Hubert, and, informed that Arthur lives, he speaks no more of conscience (IV.2).

Difficult to act perhaps, this kind of John nevertheless seems more faithful to Shakespeare's text than the mother's boy of recent productions. John's character retains its opacity, but the Bastard's choric commentary works with such an approach rather than in contrast to it. The Bastard's relationship in the first three acts, therefore, must be primarily with the audience; everyone on stage already knows what he tells us: that everything can be made to serve politics and that politics is a game of competing self-interests. The savage farce of history saddens us even as it amuses and disgusts us, and in *King John* a few of the characters share these Shakespearean feelings and perceptions as well. Some critics have seen *King John* as the darkest of the English history plays, as "the most cynical and disillusioned,"[11] as "the most discomforting and disconcerting."[12] John's consciousness of the meanness of his unprincipled machinations forms part of that darkness, though it can hardly raise him to tragic stature. In John's requesting Hubert to kill Arthur, Swinburne saw this element of the play's darkness in John's hesitations, in "the shapeless and miscreated birth of a murderous purpose that labours into light even while it loathes the light and itself."[13]

This scene of John's urging Arthur's murder seriously diminishes whatever kingliness John has possessed and marks the turning point in his fortunes. Its counterpart later in the court scene (IV.2) in which Pembroke, Salisbury, and the other nobles "burn in indignation" (103) over Arthur's supposed death reveals that John all along has been facing a "no-win" situation: Arthur alive provides the Barons a focus for just rebellion against the usurper; Arthur dead at John's instigation provides a cause for revolt. John has always been trapped in his "borrowed majesty," and the concatenation of threats must inevitably extend into the doomed future of John's reign. Here in this scene, the "ill tidings" multiply at a "giddy pace," as Shakespeare takes events scattered over a period from 1200 to 1216 and makes them occur simultaneously. John's nobles, indignant at the report of Arthur's death, leave the court, promising not to bear this criminality. A messenger reports that the French have arrived on English shores and that Eleanor is dead. John pleads with Fortune for time: "Withhold thy speed, dreadful

occasion!" (125), but the Bastard enters to report the strange fantasies, rumors, idle dreams, and fears of the people and to relate the
prophecy of Peter of Pomfret that John shall "deliver up" his crown
before the next Ascension Day. In the space of fifty lines, John's
control has been shattered, and with Hubert's re-entrance a sixth
blow falls upon the staggered king: the five moons upon which the
common people "prophesy . . . dangerously" (186).

The theatrical effectiveness of this series of blows should be
clear in performance. The "policy" of expediency has drawn the
net tighter, generating more indignation and fear than security.
Yet even here John does not collapse: he sends the Bastard after
the nobles to win back their love and, with Hubert's report that
Arthur lives, he regains hope and orders Hubert after the "angry
lords" as well. The next time John appears, he is yielding his crown
to Rome in order to receive it again from Pandulph, a last desperate
charade to forestall foreign invasion and discontent at home by
using Pandulph's influence to call off the French. Again, a series
of bad news follows: Pandulph reminds him that it is Ascension
Day; the Bastard enters with the report that nothing remains in
their power save Dover Castle and that the lords have found
Arthur dead; and John must endure the encouragements of the
Bastard's string of imperatives to "be great in act" (V.1.43–50)
and his disgust with this "inglorious league" with Rome (65).
The explicit stage directions in the Bastard's speech call for John
to look beaten – a sad, drooping, collapsed monarch who can only
respond by curtly abdicating his role: "Have thou the ordering of
this present time" (77). John has only one other short scene before
his death, and there he cannot even welcome the "good news" that
Lewis's supply ships "Are wrack'd three nights ago on Goodwin
Sands" (V.3.15). Again, Shakespeare has huddled together events
widely spaced over fifteen years in his historical sources.

John is not all wickedness and weakness; he is a man trapped by
circumstances to which his own machinations and the fickleness of
Fortune contribute. The play itself becomes partly the tragedy of
England, partly the moral spectacle of John's inevitable ruin, yet
any assertion that John becomes admirable or tragic goes too far
to the other extreme from condemning him completely.[14] John dies
without remorse or expiation: he complains only of the torments
of the body and says nothing of the soul or conscience. Even
the "clod / And module of confounded royalty" he calls himself
(V.7.57–58) seems but a physical image, not a cry of remorse. The

audience throughout the play remains quite detached from John; our emotional responses are directed elsewhere: to the fascination of the Bastard's bluntness and wit, the pathos of Arthur's innocence, and the grief and madness of Constance's motherly love. Yet these characters, rather than drawing our attention away from the moral spectacle of John's power politics, contribute to our seeing it more clearly. There are no heroes, only victims, some villainous, some innocent, and there are few survivors.

THE POLITICAL LANGUAGE OF EXCESS

In a play so full of victims, one is not surprised to encounter an abundance of pathos; in a world so full of self-interest, one is not surprised to find so much irony. Constance's grief and Arthur's innocence are, of course, chiefly responsible for the pathetic element, and the Bastard's soliloquies and asides for the comic, satirical, and ironic elements; yet each adds to the other: the tirades of Constance and the disinterestedness of Arthur sharply criticize the unprincipled actions of the kings and Pandulph; the Bastard's outrage, sorrow, and confusion intensifies the pathos. Although modern taste spurns the pathetic, because of it *John* held its place in the select repertoire of Shakespearean plays in the eighteenth and nineteenth centuries. Between 1737 and 1823 it was produced in thirty-eight seasons in London,[15] and Henry Irving's biographer places it among only ten other plays frequently performed.[16] Even the often hostile George Bernard Shaw, who had found *King John* boring and "insufferably tedious" in the study, having seen Tree's production, pronounced it "a really fine play."[17] Its successes as theater may be partly attributed to specific performers and to the spectacle of costuming and stage design, but these elements belong to the medium; short of interpolation of scenes and of adaptations – Tree inserted a tableau of the Magna Carta being granted; Buzz Goodbody added scenes from *The Troublesome Raigne*; Barton rewrote the whole play, adding his own scenes as well as material from the *Raigne* and from Bale's *King Johan* – defining what is extratextual always becomes difficult.

Of the major characters apart from King John, Lewis and Pandulph provide variations upon the hollow rhetoric and unprincipled action of hardboiled politics. Arthur and Hubert remain essentially passive characters: Arthur the innocent, indifferent, but

legitimate heir; Hubert progressing from neutrality to loyalty to
John and almost to a venial criminality, carried along by events
beyond his control. Constance and the Bastard each comment upon
the amorality of politics; Constance frenziedly lamenting the farce
of political maneuvering – the breaches of faith, the masquerade of
self-interest as law – and the Bastard for almost four acts learning
more and more complex lessons in *Realpolitik* and providing the
audience a perspective outside the action. Each of these six reveals
the multifaceted simplicity of the play's "mad world" of politics,
and each does so in ways visually and rhetorically distinctive and
highly theatrical. The visual staging owes something to the morality
tradition, and the characters' language, rather than a jumble of
pathos and rant, often supports the visual histrionics and forms
almost a subplot in which competing rhetorics and styles engage
in their own linguistic politics. The play is about excess, and the
various styles contribute to the politics of excess.[18] Rhetorical excess
in some scenes literally acts out the characters' emotional excesses
and in others reminds us of the artificiality of what we are seeing:
this is a play upon the stage of history upon the stage in the theater
in which we are seated. The Bastard most obviously contributes
to demolishing the masquerades of diplomacy, but others, less
self-consciously, undermine themselves through their own fustian,
heroic, casuistic, and otherwise hollow language.

Act II, Scene 1, provides a good example. As with the first
tetralogy, ceremony becomes dramatic when shattered. The scene
is structured around rhetorical and dramaturgical symmetries:
balanced staging of opposing parties, speeches of approximately
the same length, paired exits and re-entrances, and so forth. But
the seriousness becomes farce as the ironies pile up, as Hubert
refuses admittance to the city of Angiers to any but the English
king, once he has "proven" his title; as Constance and Eleanor
trade insults; and as the Bastard explodes the entire solemnity of
war as an extension of political diplomacy by suggesting the two
opposing forces join in destroying "this peevish town." From the
scene's opening, the doings of power seem suspect as Arthur is
forced to embrace the proud Austria, who killed his uncle, Richard
the Lionhearted, and who apparently wear's a lion's skin, and
who kisses Arthur on the cheek in vowing to support his claims.
The audience would recognize a stage emblem in this embrace,
accompanied by Constance's "mother's thanks" (32) to the "fair
boy" (30, 43) and surrounded by more experienced, pragmatic,

self-interested foreign powers – Philip the French king and the lion-skinned Austria. There follows Chatillon's report of John's speed and then John's arrival. In the midst of the discussion of lineal right, Eleanor and Constance trade abuses, adding to the talk of "usurp'd authority" (118–21), one of the play's major themes, and the Bastard threatens Austria with a violent undressing of his "skin-coat" (139). Lewis must interrupt these confused shouting matches – "Women and fools, break off your conference" (150) – to return this farce to diplomatic ceremony. But to no avail: Arthur tries – "Good my mother, peace!" (163) – and John tries – "Bedlam, have done!" (183) – and Philip tries – "Peace, lady!" (195). Constance's emotional intensity exposes the formal posturings of opponents and allies alike. Should not an audience laugh at their failures and at her witty, emotional repartees as she picks up a word from Eleanor's one-liners, elaborates it, plays with it, twists bad conceits from it? The intemperance of Constance approaches farce, and as it does, the scene returns to the "normality" of the siege of Angiers. Hubert appears upon the upper stage to hear John's and Philip's almost symmetrical, lengthy speeches, advancing their lawful right and threatening annihilation, a curious combination, to be sure. Hubert recognizes neither argument, promising only to "prove loyal" to "he that proves the king" (270–71), and the Bastard comments that each party is full of bastards. The latter series of asides makes the audience share the Bastard's perspective and see these proceedings as so much false heroics:

> Saint George, that swing'd the dragon, and e'er since
> Sits on's horse-back at mine hostess' door,
> Teach us some fence!
>
> (II.1.287–89)

Constance and the Bastard perform similar functions in ironically deflating the artifice in this heroic and rhetorical farce. The play's principals have great difficulty in silencing the hecklers in their on-stage audience.

After the symmetrical exits of the English and French parties, symmetrical excursions, trumpets, speeches by English and French heralds, and re-entrances by the kings, the "scroyles of Angiers" still cannot decide upon the King of England. The Bastard suggests the "wild counsel" of their joining forces and levelling Angiers. That his suggestion meets with immediate approval from both John and

Philip underlines the savage farce of politics, the Machiavellian disregard for principle. "Smacks it not something of the policy?" asks the Bastard (396). Hubert's alternative to Angiers' destruction – the diplomatic marriage of Lewis and Blanche – rounds out this escalation of "policy," attiring it in the dress of love, beauty, virtue, and birth, a rhetoric of "perfection" that far exceeds even the Bastard's expectations of expedient politics:

> Here's a stay
> That shakes the rotten carcass of old death
> Out of his rage! Here's a large mouth indeed,
> That spits forth death and mountains, rocks and seas,
> Talks as familiarly of roaring lions,
> As maids of thirteen do of puppy-dogs!
> What cannoneer begot this lusty blood?
> He speaks plain cannon, fire, and smoke, and bounce;
> He gives the bastinado with his tongue;
> Our ears are cudgell'd; not a word of his
> But buffets better than a fist of France.
> Zounds! I was never so bethump'd with words
> Since I first call'd my brother's father dad.
>   (II.1.455–67)

So King Philip and the Dauphine receive the French provinces, except for the city of Angiers, as Blanche's dowry instead of fighting to win them for Arthur – a nice bargain. Lewis's hackneyed Petrarchan conceits arouse the Bastard's ridicule; both the stylized formality and its transparent emptiness prompt his aside, and his "hang'd and drawn and quarter'd" image also underlines the traitorousness of abandoning Arthur. The kings try to devise a scheme for placating Constance, in whose "right" the French "came," but which, Philip admits, "we, God knows, have turn'd another way / To our own vantage" (550). Temporarily, everything has been solved, and the parties "haste" toward "this unlook'd for, unprepared pomp" (559–60), leaving the Bastard onstage for his long commentary.

No one has tried to conceal anything. The kings have turned from right to advantage, and the powerful seem to have no need for masks in *King John*. The formality alone apparently suffices to elevate John's buying off the French with five provinces and thirty thousand marks from self-interest to statesmanship. The competing styles turn these proceedings from epic to farce: at the extremes of formality – the heroic style of the Heralds' commands, for example, or the courtly rhetoric of Lewis's love – the action unfolds around the central plotters of siege, war, and marriage, while the peripheral and powerless Constance and the Bastard expose its hollowness in styles which mock this ceremoniousness, in Constance's playing with words and in the Bastard's ridicule. Constance's outrage is well complemented by the Bastard's detached sarcasm, and neither will be silenced so that the farce of politics may proceed. The Bastard's physical detachment from the stage groupings of the main actors would also suggest an odd exception to the formal symmetries of the dramaturgy. The scene need not be played for laughs to bring out its comic elements; once again, the breaking of ceremony forms the dramatic common denominator in Shakespeare's approach to the heroic postures in the early history plays.[19] Even without the pointing asides of the Bastard, the overdone rhetoric of the royal parties dramatizes a parody of politics, which is clear enough in the long stretches of the scene in which the Bastard has nothing to say but is present on the stage.

Morality play dramaturgy adds to the visual thematics of this scene and is complemented by some strikingly vivid personifications. King Philip here – and again in Act III – plays the morality role of the King pulled in both directions by Expediency (King John) and by Right (Constance); that these characters fail to be simple Good and Bad Angels does not undermine this essential structure but rather highlights it.[20] In his soliloquy, the Bastard iterates this stage emblem, underlining Philip's abandoned role as God's deputy, the King:

> And France, whose armour conscience buckled on,
> Whom zeal and charity brought to the field
> As God's own soldier, rounded in the ear
> With that same purpose-changer, that sly divel,
> What broker, that still breaks the pate of faith,
> That daily break-vow, he that wins of all,
> Of kings, of beggars, old men, young men, maids . . .
> That smooth-fac'd gentleman, tickling commodity . . .
>   (II.1.564–73)

Whispering temptations in the King's ear, forcing him from the religious virtues – conscience, zeal, and charity – which would accompany Philip to an "honourable war" (585), "That sly divel" surely comes from the morality play tradition to sum up the scene effectively in the guise of the sportive, Vice-like "Commodity." That there will be no Good Hope and Sad Circumspection to save these wayward kings adds to the complex use of morality play materials and images.

The Bastard himself has been described as playing "the morality play role of Simplicity."[21] The play clearly dramatizes his progress from naivete to cynicism to confusion to patriotism – an education in political reality which structurally, though not thematically, resembles those of a number of late moralities and interludes. Perhaps he can best be seen as a central figure in *John* by recalling the essentially passive nature of such recipients of a political education in plays such as Skelton's *Magnificence* or *The Interlude of Youth*. That there occur many of their visual and linguistic structures has perhaps obscured this element of *John*. What Shakespeare has done as well is to see the impossibility of choosing rightly between the apparent morality play options. From the beginning when the Bastard must choose between Wealth – five hundred twelfth-century pounds a year definitely qualifies as a temptation – and Honor, characters face choices among options which combine both good and evil.[22] The religious dimensions appear only to be treated lightly but their presence nevertheless underlines their powerlessness; the Bastard concludes his meditation upon that "divel," Commodity:

> Well, whiles I am a beggar, I will rail
> And say there is no sin but to be rich;
> And being rich, my virtue then shall be
> To say there is no vice but beggary.
> Since kings break faith upon commodity,
> Gain, be my lord, for I will worship thee!
> (II.1.593–98)

All parties are implicated in this worship of "gain," another name for the devil of self-advantage – including John, with his thirty thousand "Bastards and else" (276), who has traded a part of his usurped kingdom in order to "stop Arthur's title in the whole" (562).

Pandulph's joining the dispute reopens the hostilities and prompts another stage emblem which owes something to the

morality play tradition. John and Philip stand in the center of the
stage, holding hands for a very long time – at least from line 118 to
188 – an image of peace and courtesy – while Eleanor urges Philip
not to "let go thy hand" (121), and Pandulph, Constance, Austria,
and Lewis counsel vehemently the letting go and breaking of the
peace in favor of avoiding Rome's curse and furthering another
war. Lewis's advice perhaps offers the most obvious example of
self-interest:

> Bethink you, father: for the difference
> Is purchase of a heavy curse from Rome,
> Or the light loss of England for a friend:
> Forgo the easier.
> (III.1.130–33)

Again, the morality play structure is made clear, this time by
Constance, who answers Eleanor:

> Look to that, devil, lest that France repent,
> And by disjoining hands, hell lose a soul.
> (122–23)

Meanwhile, the Bastard is punctuating this solemnity with the
refrain, "And hang a calve's skin on his recreant limbs" (125, 146,
225), and Pandulph, representative of "the church, our mother," is
urging war and breaking vows in the most casuistical double-talk:

> What since thou swor'st is sworn against thyself
> And may not be performed by thyself,
> For that which thou hast sworn to do amiss
> Is not amiss when it is truly done,
> And being not done, where doing tends to ill,
> The truth is then most done not doing it:
> The better act of purposes mistook
> Is to mistake again; though indirect,
> Yet indirection thereby grows direct,
> And falsehood falsehood cures, as fire cools fire
> Within the scorch'd veins of one new-burn'd.
> It is religion that doth make vows kept,
> But thou hast sworn against religion:

By what thou swear'st against the thing thou swear'st,
And mak'st an oath the surety for thy truth!
Against an oath the truth thou art unsure
To swear – swears only not to be forsworn!
Else what a mockery should it be to swear?
But thou dost swear only to be forsworn,
And most forsworn, to keep what thou dost swear.
Therefore . . . .

(III.1.194–214)

Pandulph's speech approaches broad comedy: who cannot be amused by the ceremonious formality of the two hand-holding kings dropping their alliance to listen to this? Moreover, on one side, Austria and the Bastard squabble, and, on the other, Blanche laments her wedding-day's feast, falls to her knees, and begs for peace. The drawing-and-quartering conceit of the Bastard's ridicule of Lewis's lover's rhetoric has become the reality of Blanche's sorrow; the dropping of the handshake becomes the variation of hands pulling her apart:

Which is the side that I must go withal?
I am with both: each army hath a hand;
And in their rage, I having hold of both,
They whirl asunder and dismember me.

(253–56)

Blanche illustrates the impossibility of anyone's winning at this match; among the women on stage in this scene she stands as Innocence between the twin representations of Ambition, Eleanor and Constance.

The following scenes move away from these morality play influences toward a different kind of theatricality. The Bastard opens III.2 carrying Austria's head and lays it on the stage, an action as likely to arouse laughter as to evoke shock and reminiscent of Richard Crookback at the beginning of *3 Henry VI*. In fact, to avoid laughter John Philip Kemble in 1814 replaced Austria's head with Falconbridge's entrance in the lion's skin Austria had been wearing previously, and this stage practice enjoyed a considerable longevity.[23] But this laughter appears to be exactly the intended reaction from the audience: Austria has been a joke all along, a blustering braggart, and now the Bastard for the first time has actually entered into the action of the plot by doing and not merely by talking.

The Bastard is sent off to ransack the coffers of the "hoarding abbots"; Eleanor, newly rescued by the Bastard, takes aside Arthur, newly captured; and John makes his proposal to Hubert. Readers might need reminding that Arthur, although out of the range of hearing their conversation, remains onstage throughout this pivotal exchange, innocent of what is being plotted in his presence. The pathos of the later scenes is being prepared for, and no doubt Arthur's presence intensifies the grimness and cruelty. However John's role is played, the scene is effective theater.[24] John paints the scene black with a string of "if" clauses which transform the sunny pleasant day into a still night that will not allow him and Hubert to see each other's faces – a churchyard at the dead of night whose dark silence is broken by an imaginary "midnight bell" (III.2.44–65). The language creates the visual emblem which is absent from the actual scene; what we do see is John and Hubert together and Eleanor apart with Arthur. The midnight churchyard and the staging leave us in no doubt about the evil of this usurper.

Shakespeare makes language complement the stage images at the most theatrical moments. Often it has been this imagery which has drawn the most positive critical comments about *King John*. Caroline Spurgeon, for example, sees many of the descriptive speeches as providing "a kind of illumination or decorative marginal gloss to the play, a series of tiny allegorical pictures, dancing with life and movement, which far from lessening the vigor of reality, as allegory sometimes does, increase its vividness and poignancy tenfold,"[25] E. A. J. Honigmann, the Arden editor, asserts that the "repeating symbols," such as the images of distortion and deformity, and the "perpetual personifications," such as those of Death and Fortune, "almost achieve the stature of dramatis personae."[26] Both comments point to the nature of the functions of language and style in the play: to bring out the darkness of the radically unstable jungle of politics and the liveliness of the world apart from it. The Bastard's Death "feasts, mousing the flesh of men" with "fangs" made of the "swords of soldiers" (II.1.352–54), and Constance calls upon Death the "carrion monster":

> Death! death, O amiable, lovely Death!
> Thou odoriferous stench! sound rottenness!
> Arise forth from the couch of lasting night,

> Thou hate and terror to prosperity,
> And I will kiss thy detestable bones
> And put my eyeballs in thy vaulty brows . . .
>   (III.3.25–30)

Wishing to take Death as a husband, the grieving Constance through her emotional excesses demonstrates that Death, along with War and Fortune, governs this world. Again, as in II.1, the politicians – this time Philip and Pandulph – try in vain to silence her. The language of her extreme, frenzied grief complements the stage image she turns herself into: the hair-tearing, dishevelled, screaming Fury. Constance's language is excessive because emotion and words are all she has left. She stands powerless and abject before the two leaders of France and Rome who have not only failed her and allowed Arthur to be captured but also now call her grief madness, counsel patience, tell her to bind up her tresses, and generally belittle her sorrow. After her personification of Grief as Arthur's changeling (93–97), Constance leaves the stage, never to return; our last image of her is meant to sum up her powerlessness which includes the power of language to move an audience's emotions and its impotence in this political world if not allied with sources of real power.

Juxtaposed with Constance's pathos, Pandulph's self-damning sophistries, and the kings' self-serving rhetoric, the Bastard's style appears natural, energetic, and straightforward. It gives the play what comedy it has beyond the intended bathos of ironic fustian, but it also fills in the political world with the everyday detail of common life. The effect most often is to deflate the ceremoniousness of politics, to diminish the players of this game, as in these personifications when Hubert picks up Arthur's corpse:

> The life, the right and truth of all this realm
> Is fled to heaven; and England now is left
> To tug and scamble, and to part by th' teeth
> The unow'd interest of proud swelling state.
> Now for the bare-pick'd bone of majesty
> Doth dogged war bristle his angry crest
> And snarleth in the gentle eyes of peace:
> Now powers from home and discontents at home
> Meet in one line; and vast confusion waits,
> As doth a raven on a sick-fall'n beast . . . .
>   (IV.3.144–53)

His function in the first two-thirds is to comment sarcastically upon the participants' self-interested game-playing, but most often his analysis introduces into the margins of this world of kings the powerless common people who never actually mount this stage: the traveller with his toothpick (I.1.190), the gaping, pointing theatergoers (II.1.375), the maids of thirteen talking of puppy dogs (460), the bawd Commodity, who is a familiar Elizabethan type in many ways (582), Time, that "bald sexton" (III.1.250), hundreds of citizens at the heels of Peter the Prophet of Pomfret (IV.2.149), the smith with his hammer and the tailor in his slippers (IV.2.193), the beardless dandy in silks (V.1.70), "boyish troops" (V.2.133), "pale-visaged maids" (154), among a wealth of others. All these add to the "felt life" of *John* as well as to the farce of a few men's self-interests; the common folk literally inhabit the margins of this world though the center of Falconbridge's consciousness.

The Bastard anticipates Falstaff in his mastery of styles. He himself calls attention to the necessity of detecting the deceit of "Exterior form, outward accoutrement" (I.1.211) and consistently mocks the styles of the others. In his own quick verse-making, he produces three rhyming sestets, the first of which in stringing together proverbs in a witty manner states his identity apart from lineage: "I am I, howe'er I was begot" (I.1.175). The second wittily reverses traditional values – for Lady Falconbridge, his mother, not to have been an adultress would have been a sin – and the third mocks Lewis's love rhetoric with Blanche. In addition, in the first two acts the Bastard has a dozen or more couplets, whose purpose most often is to undermine the stuffy formality of the other characters and to stress his quickness and adaptability. Having established his levity and wit, Shakespeare drops the rhymes, using only the traditional scene-ending couplets in the last three acts. However, the Bastard's rhetorical capacity serves him well in imitation rather than mockery when he speaks better than John himself could in threatening Lewis in the grand heroic style (V.2.128 ff.). Paradoxically, the audience can accept the Armada rhetoric from the Bastard here and at the end of the play because he has so thoroughly exposed its hypocrisy in the language of the others.

In the complementarity of plotting, staging, and language, *King John* offers a highly theatrical melodrama of political history. What seems flat in reading appears on stage as part of a rhythm of rises and falls, successes and failures, which has a succession of

turning points in the middle of the play. The off-and-on alliance
of Constance, Philip, Austria, and sometimes Pandulph perhaps
best demonstrates the shifting, unstable personal interests of John's
world; for Constance the capture of Arthur leads to her hysterical finale of passion (III.3). John's manipulations escalate from
machiavellian expediency to a murderous behest (III.2). Arthur's
innocence is put in its greatest danger with Hubert's executioners
and hot irons (IV.1), climaxing a series of stage pictures of Arthur's
powerlessness: receiving Austria's "zealous kiss" (II.1.19), urging
his mother's silence (163), standing hand-in-hnad with Philip before
Angiers (236), pleading with his mother to "be content" (II.2.42),
saying absolutely nothing through the whole of III.1 and standing
silent and apart as John orders his death in III.2 (a scene of 355
lines). He has little to say before his scene with Hubert, but his
presence on the stage forms part of the dark picture of John's
world. This scene also marks another shift in Hubert, who has
gone from neutrality to loyalty to murder to compassion. Though
our greater sympathies lie with the victimized Arthur and though
we too would not mind escaping this "iron age" (60) and – like
Henry VI – tending sheep (17), Hubert's backing away from
blinding and murdering Arthur also marks an emotional turning
point of sorts; just as the three nameless servants in *King Lear* object
to Gloucester's blinding and fetch him "flax and whites of eggs" for
his bleeding eyes (III.7.106), Hubert turns away from the "wisdom"
of expedient politics.

These scenes and those that follow – the rush of bad news for
John (IV.2) and Arthur's death and the nobles' debate (IV.3)
– offer no large-scale ensemble scenes in which all the major
characters are on stage at once – such as the deposition scene
in *Richard II*, for example – but they do work effectively. Again
in IV.2, the contrast of styles effectively underlines the instability
of this political world. Arthur begins the scene by jumping from
"the walls" to his death. Dressed as a ship-boy, his corpse lies
on stage throughout the scene until Hubert carries it off at the
end. Discovering his body, Salisbury, Pembroke, and the Bastard
lament his death and its cause; in these responses the styles tell the
audience whose sincerity to trust:

> *Salis.* Sir Richard, what think you? You have beheld.
> Or have you read, or heard? or could you think,
> Or do you almost think, although you see,

That you do see? could thought, without this object,
Form such another? This is the very top,
The heighth, the crest, or crest unto the crest,
Of murther's arms: this is the bloodiest shame,
The wildest savagery, the vildest stroke,
That ever wall-ey'd wrath or staring rage
Presented to the tears of remorse.
   Pemb. All murthers past do stand excus'd in this:
And this, so sole and unmatchable,
Shall give a holiness, a purity,
To the yet unbegotten sin of times;
And to prove a deadly bloodshed but a jest,
Exampled by the heinous spectacle.
   Bast. It is a damned and bloody work;
The graceless action of a heavy hand,
If that it be the work of any hand.
(41–59)

The Bastard and the play have taught us to be skeptical of such excesses in language, and the succinct response more aptly expresses grief and outrage. Whatever John's crimes may be, Salisbury and Pembroke are just so much more chaff blown by the winds of advantage: they will return for the very last scene to comfort Prince Henry at his father's death (V.2.75) and tender their love and support to the new king (106). Their very presence warrants the audience's suspicion of the ending's promises of a patriotic unity and a restored peace. Though Salisbury cries at the thought of marching "after a stranger" upon England's "gentle bosom" (V.2.28), Lewis comforts him with "the purse of rich prosperity" he will share with the other nobles (61). This "earthquake of nobility" no doubt represents the tragic divisions of the discontented barons and becomes a theatrical embodiment of the shifts of allegiance in the last two acts, yet clearly self-interest rules as Salisbury opts for the spoils of war and Lewis double-crosses them all, ordering them recompensed with death (V.4.15).

By simple elimination, the Bastard becomes the only sympathetic character left. Although he achieves some stature as England's savior, his luck – good and bad – appears as important as his military prowess in his gaining the temporary control with which the play concludes. The weakness of *King John* as a play lies mostly in this last act. One cannot deny the Bastard's centrality nor his heroic leadership, but the effective scenes of the first four acts yield to long rhetorical speeches and various reports upon the status of battles. The act begins with the very perfunctory ceremony of the re-crowning of John and ends with the war petering out though by no means over. In the reports, most of the influential events involve accidents or miscalculations rather than heroic exploits: the wreck of the French supply ships on the Goodwin Sands or the loss of half the Bastard's power in the Lincoln Washes. Surely, the dramatist means these accidents as more deflation of the heroic world of the chronicles, as examples of the power of Fortune, and as the continued shifting of allegiances; perhaps we should see the "vast confusion" the Bastard predicts (IV.3.152) in the rapid changes of Act V.

King John, in any case, cannot be reduced to the patriotism of its last speeches, nor can it be seen as primarily a warning against rebellion, whatever its textual and topical meanings. The Bastard's kneeling before Prince Henry and speaking of "faithful services / And true subjection" provides an image of loyalty to a higher principle than self-interest. He states a noble ideal and does so without surrendering his perspicacity, but the audience has just seen how this national unity was achieved: with the help of accidents at sea, Melun's warning the nobles of Lewis's intentions, and a monk's poisons removing the usurping king. The hope and the noble sentiments add light to the darkness of the political jungle, and perhaps restoring the "lineal state and glory of the land" (102) is what we count on language to do.

When the Bastard accepts and masters the rhetoric of excess at the end of *King John*, he does so not as the cynical manipulator of the hollow language of politics but as the pragmatic spokesman of king and nation, as the courtier-statesman using imperfect resources of power. After the Bastard's sarcastic exposure of the illusions of power and authority, such an informed pragmatism recognizes and embraces the flawed nature of the political world and anticipates Prince Hal's conscious self-education in the language and theatricality of kingship and his creating and performing his own drama on the stage of history.

7
Paradox, Play, Politics

As a practical man of theater, as actor turned playwright, as the only English Renaissance dramatist to spend his entire career within the theatrical establishment, Shakespeare owed his allegiances as a writer first to his company and his audience, and those were to create theatrically exciting plays. To a growing number of recent scholars, seeing his plays as opposing or contesting the dominant ideological positions of his day suggests reassessing traditional conceptions of Shakespeare, but we need not replace an orthodox or conservative playwright with an adversarial one, openly and consistently subversive. The early history plays themselves warn us against conclusions and invite us to explore instead the paradoxes, to think about the nature of Shakespeare's theater rather than "Shakespeare's politics."

These chapters have tried to extend the critical tasks of understanding the theatrical dimensions of these plays. Interpreting dramatic texts as plays also involves locating their theatricality within other symbolic and theatrical structures of the Elizabethan political culture and within a heightened awareness of the implications of the public stage as an institution whose practices intersect and comment upon the ideological presentations of that culture. Without question, the plays of the second tetralogy provide us with a much more profound and far greater dramatic exploration of the theatricalism of politics, but in the Henry VI plays, *Richard III*, and *King John* Shakespeare discovered the dramatic potential of the serious practical matters implicit in his sources, in the contradictions inherent in political life, and the discrepancies and disjunctions between the ceremonial, theatrical, and rhetorical displays of power and authority and the political and military realities they mystify or ignore. Most often, these plays disclose the partiality of competing explanations of political events, human motives, and historical circumstances, on the one hand, exposing the ironies which challenge their interpretive completeness and

147

certainty but, on the other hand, presenting the competition fully and, most often, as part of the paradoxes at play on the political stages of history. That is, politics as paradox insists upon the "both/and" of contradiction, upon what A. P. Rossiter called the "two-eyed" view, an "ambivalence" which subsumes two opposed judgments or explanations without invalidating or discrediting either.[1] What magnifies this sense of politics as paradox are the reverberations of one paradox as it impinges upon or confronts another; from these connections the complexities of history become nearly inexhaustible for either the dramatist or the interpreter of history. "Paradox," in this sense, is not merely or essentially the inevitable language that great poetry uses; the history plays explore the paradoxes inherent in the political culture and in the nature of representing it on the public stage.

One constellation of paradoxes revolves around the dualities of the monarch. The king is fixed in the iconic, institutional, and ideological presentational politics of unchanging structures, the display of his power and authority governed by traditions of ceremony and language whose flexibility is limited. In a sense, the king exists in the timeless world of meaning, as the resilient doctrine of the "king's (or queen's) two bodies" suggests. Yet the king must also respond to the vicissitudes of change, the restless ambitions of barons or courtiers, the discontent of his subjects, and all the other problems blown his way by the winds of time. In the late 1580s and early 1590s, the conditions in Elizabethan England could only have highlighted the divisions between iconic and historical, display and reality, as the Virgin Queen aged along with her carefully perfected self-presentations, as the precarious complications of factional, parliamentary, and religious opposition undermined the picture of order, as wars in Ireland and on the Continent belied the rhetoric of peace, as rising food prices, bad harvests, higher taxes, and peasant revolts undermined the langauge of plenty and prosperity.

The paradox of ceremony equally exposes and disguises not only the monarch but all those to whom the liturgy of state assigns roles. Though Henry V understands this paradox better than other Shakespearean kings, from the opening scene of 1 *Henry VI* and throughout the other four earlier plays, the masks of ceremony reveal and hide true motive.[2] Ceremony forces its participants to assume the traditional behavior required by their roles for the static, ritual conduct of the ceremony to go forward, but provides a ready means for concealing private passions inimical to the orderly administration of power and privilege. The iconic is heavily dependent upon the ceremonial; the historical inevitably violates it, sooner or later, as the roles cease to be concordant with changed circumstances or the ambitious reject their assigned roles in the hierarchy or those treated inequitably desire to alter the liturgy. Henry VI's attempts at monarchical ceremony formally obey the traditional rites of instantiating the iconic meanings of kingship within the historic moment, yet they also prove absolutely futile since the disloyal lords and later the ambitious Yorks no longer accept the roles assigned. Ceremonial display often expects tradition to convey the naturalness of the present order; it itself does not necessarily legitimize power and authority but opens the legitimacy of the present order to review and possibly dispute.

The paradox of theatrical politics is closely related to these problems of rule and ceremony. In a sense, presentational displays of power must necessarily suggest the vulnerability, weakness, incompleteness, or even absence of power.[3] The dark side of Elizabeth's theatrical politics might be illustrated by the punishment of Stubbs, the execution of the Babington conspirators, or by a number of other highly visible enactments of state justice on the stage of the public scaffold. Cases such as those of John Stubbs, who lost a hand for opposing a marriage which the Queen herself rejected, or of Roderigo Lopez, her Spanish physician and a converted Jew, who was hanged and dismembered for attempting to poison his sovereign, reveal the paradoxicality of such public spectacles: whether the opponents of power are inventions of subversion to display the power of the crown to contain dissent and violence or truly rebellious and criminal threats to order, the spectacle of public justice opens itself to interpretation and response. To present the image of ideological harmony and unity, one must first present (or sometimes misrepresent) the forces of discontent and opposition which must be silenced or transformed, those very sources of conflict which the best interests of ideology would wish to remain hidden. If one represents the war's disabled or masterless men as dangerous, they may come to believe that they are and act accordingly, the feared becoming fearsome, the demonized demons; on the other hand, one may cry, "God save the Queen," as Stubbs did, or die maintaining that one "loved the Queene as well as Christ Jesus," as did Lopez, and radically alter the script.

Elizabeth's awareness of the dangers and paradoxes of politics as performance was acute. Her famous remark – "we Princes are set as it were upon Stages in the Sight and view of all the World" – forms part of her answer to Parliament's request that she take center stage and preside over the trial of Mary Queen of Scots, justifies her theatrical absence from the proceedings, and probably anticipates the vehemence of her response to news of her execution. On the lighter side, the chivalric and pastoral masquerades, the Petrarchan politics of the Court, and the endless multiplication of mythological associations evidence a playful self-consciousness which includes more fantasy and charm than it contains subversion. Elizabeth could mock her own histrionic prowess as an actress upon the stage of politics while glorying in it, could regret the privileged visibility of the monarch while insisting upon it and exploiting it. She tried to turn the vulnerability of her position as a female sovereign of a patriarchal state into an asset, but her successes remained fragile fictions. Her encouraging courtiers, playwrights, and poets to woo her had the effect of discouraging clear demarcations between literary and political discourse, and, to a great extent, her aestheticizing of politics had the paradoxical consequence of politicizing aesthetics. Indeed, political, literary, theological, social, scientific, legal, commercial, and sexual metaphors were all drawn from an undifferentiated, uncompartmentalized language which recognized few distinctions or conjunctures among subject matters.[4] Moreover, because the Court, unlike the isolated and incomprehensible circle of favorites around the Stuart kings, was open and accessible to the aristocracy, interested in the theatrical community, and both visible and intelligible to the public, politics and public stage reciprocally promoted an interest in, perhaps even a preoccupation with, presentations of government and power.[5]

We need not turn the early histories into hunting grounds for topicality, into direct reflections of contemporary political issues – "mirrors of Elizabethan policy," but the theatrical politics of late sixteenth-century England surely heightened many of the paradoxes of rule. What we now call the ideological, iconic, and institutional would seem to those sensitive to image and language less and less grounded in the natural and divine order of things and more and more aesthetic and social, fictions motivated by historical and pragmatic politics. The official positions – the authority of genealogical succession, the monarch as God's deputy, the providentialism of the Tudors' ending the Wars of the Roses, for example – became part of the aesthetics of politics, part of the politics of aesthetics. The language which legitimized power and privilege could be seen as another facet of the self-consciousness of theatrical politics. One paradox of the theater in general and of the history play in particular is that it can only represent. From this conservative perspective, the public stage is inevitably subversive, since it will not allow the premise that the monarch presents himself, the actor re-presents the monarch. The Puritans were right: the common players in appropriating the language, costumes, and gestures of their betters, especially of the English royalty, were exposing the play-acting involved in all social convention and thereby its arbitrary rather than absolute nature. All the world's a stage: everyone appropriates something for his role; aesthetics is politics; politics is aesthetics; the distinction between stage and state collapses; all history is contemporary, since the past is appropriated for a performance in the present; politics is play, politics as play, and the play with politics: the stage is all the world.

In staging the English past, Shakespeare exploited the paradoxes of politics to dramatize fully the irony and obliquity of history. Most of the characters in these early plays unknowingly embody the blindness of acting without a sense of these paradoxes; they believe in the efficacy of law or ceremony or political ethics or violence to achieve the suppression or abrogation of the other view suspended in paradox. If man makes history, God's providence is a fiction; if God's direction of human events is real though often inscrutable, man arrogantly assumes a non-existent power to alter the course of history. If all history is both present and past, the Tudor myth will dissolve the paradox by making the past prologue; if Richard of Gloucester triumphs in evil, he acts as the scourge of God. In political affairs the agents of making or interpreting events seem uncomfortable with the contradictions inherent in paradox, preferring to deny the opposition, to privilege one view over the other, or to absorb one view into the other. Those with enough awareness – like Richard of York or especially Richard of Gloucester – play with the contradictions, manipulating the language and the appearances of corporate values, national interests, legitimizing sanctions, and divine justifications for their own self-interest, or – like the Bastard – reconcile themselves to political life's imperfection and ironies. The first two pursue their own ambition, while the latter supports the stability of the realm, but each recognizes the necessity of masking one's personal beliefs and desires within an unavoidably Machiavellian world. Yet acting upon political exigency rather than political ethics does not always work either;

a series of repentant failures illustrate the possible failure of the pragmatic approach: Cardinal Beauford, Clarence, Hastings, Buckingham, King John, Constance, and the English earls.

Such paradoxes of power allow only the temporary expression of straightforward heroism and political morality. Each of these plays seriously compromises its major characters, and each produces its innocent victims: the chivalric and loyal Talbot in *1 Henry VI*, the admirable though ineffective Humphrey and the butchered Lords Cromer and Say in Part 2, the king himself in Part 3, the unhistorically young Rutland and the Princes in *Richard III*, the pawn Lady Blanche and Arthur, the boy who would not be king, in *John*. In the wake of *Tamburlaine* and the defeat of the Armada, Shakespeare's early history plays departed radically from the heroic drama of his predecessors and contemporaries to explore a history without heroes, a past without balladry, romance, folklore, or exotic locales. Heroism has its role to play in the early histories, one of which is to become another element of the tenuous ceremony, display, and liturgy of state. To find a formal shape within the chaos and brutality of events required a larger conception of the aesthetics of politics.

In terms of theatrical sensationalism, the plays could allow the violence of the chronicles to speak for itself in the actions dramatized. Compressing events spaced over many years into one or two scenes could help shape and highlight the paradoxes of politics. But what had to be invented and developed was the theatrical expression of the dynamic, ambivalent, ironic, and paradoxical. Flux, change, timing, randomness, human irrationality, the vicissitudes of climate, the raw violence of power, all those things which have their own roles to play upon the stage of history have – by their nature – no aesthetic form nor voice of their own. They are part of the counter-order or anti-structure of the future as it unfolds in the present; always with us, these elements cannot long be denied a central influence over the outcome of political affairs, but will not for centuries be expressed in their own imagery and ideology. Therefore, for example, to express the opposition of timeless iconic meaning and the formless unpredictability of events involved in the paradox of rule meant undermining or mutilating the images developed by those traditions in authority, violating their ceremonies, and appropriating their rhetoric. If political life was most often determined by the urgency of the moment, by physical force, personal ambition, or aristocratic factions, the pressures of political exigency demanded expression. All that failed to recognize the pragmatic and paradoxical in the making of history became vulnerable to mockery, inversion, and displacement; the dramatic structures of the political morality play and interlude and the discourses on the Christian monarch were as partial in their certainties about the kingly virtues as ceremony, dynastic historiography, and all the other modes of presentational politics were monological.

Two brief examples from the early history plays may serve to illustrate ways in which the rhetoric which legitimizes power is displaced. Though these provide but a small sampling of Shakespeare's techniques, each looks at least two ways, evoking multiple possibilities of response and interpretation as it stages the complexity of history and evidences the difficulties of interpreting the early histories.

In the following exchange, Dick the Butcher's asides mock Jack Cade's appropriation of a royal genealogy:

> *Cade.*   My father was a Mortimer, –
> *But.*   [*Aside.*] He was an honest man, and a good brick-
> layer.
> *Cade.*   My mother a Plantagenet, –
> *But.*   [*Aside.*] I knew her well; she was a midwife.
> *Cade.*   My wife descended of the Lacies, –
> *But.*   [*Aside.*] She was, indeed, a pedlar's daughter, and
> sold many laces.
>
> (*2 Henry VI*, IV.2.37–44)

The parody continues, as Cade promises to return England to prosperity and distribute his largesse to his loyal followers, and provides the audience with an absurdly comic performance of kingship, an ironic parallel to York's pursuit of the throne, and another example of Shakespeare's dramatization of the disjunction between the language which legitimizes authority and the reality which mocks such rhetoric. The effects of such displacements may be to warn us against the folly of taking too seriously the magic of blood and the other certainties with which the ideology of the ruling classes justifies its dominance, but only after we have stopped laughing. Cade himself offers a theatrical embodiment of the playful union of ideology and subversion, a union which plays with the politics of histrionic self-dramatization but which defies a solemn analysis even while it provokes questions through the travesty of political language. Some part of the audience also probably

responded to the topicality in Cade's rebellion: it reminds us of the
rising prices and peasant revolts of the late 1580s and the 1590s; it
comments, however obliquely, upon Elizabeth's genealogical right
to the throne, recurrently disputed throughout her reign and a
lively topic especially around the time of Mary Queen of Scots'
execution. On the other hand, Cade's bloody carnival reinforces
concern with the disasters of insurrection and evokes the Tudor
ideological pronouncements about order, loyalty, and stability. One
may, that is, add this comic theft of language to Cade's list of
crimes and ignore the subversiveness of this appropriation. Since
the question of Lancastrian and Yorkist genealogy claims to the
throne polarizes the aristocracy within *2 Henry VI*, this buffoon's
free access to such political rhetoric potentially manifests its tenuous grounding in any metaphysical, natural, or divine order: York
has forcefully advanced his legal claim to the throne by arguing his
better genealogy, and Cade proves an even better claimant through
his descent from the legally superior Mortimers. The play veers
off into savage farce, whose absurdities look toward the comedy
of history and whose brutalities look toward its horror.

In a less comic vein, but with more specific reference to Tudor
concerns, here is another ironic displacement, King John's response
to Pandulph's demand that he adhere to Rome's appointment of
Stephen Langton as Archbishop of Canterbury:

> What earthy name to interrogatories
> Can taste the free breath of a sacred king?
> Thou canst not, cardinal, devise a name
> So slight, unworthy and ridiculous
> To charge me to an anwer, as the pope.
> Tell him this tale; and from the mouth of England
> Add thus much more, that no Italian priest
> Shall tithe or toll in our dominions;
> But as we, under God, are supreme head,
> So under Him that great supremacy,
> Where we do reign, we will alone uphold
> Without th' assistance of a mortal hand:
> So tell the pope, all reverence set apart
> To him and his usurp'd authority.
>   (III.1.73–86)

Shakespeare's John is clearly no "sacred king" but himself a
usurper, and later he will capitulate to expediency and Rome's

"usurp'd authority" in Pandulph's recoronation. On the one hand, in having John voice the Tudor concepts of the the single source of rule, the divine right of kings, and the supremacy of the monarch over the church, Shakespeare brings into question the linguistic and theatrical display of Elizabethan power and undermines its legitimization. The realities are that the factions within the nobility, foreign alliances, dynastic marriages, the strength of armies, and the vicissitudes of weather and wind determine the success of a nation rather than theories and policies carefully devised and theologically defensible. How much emphasis are we to place upon such ironic defamiliarizations of Tudor ideology? Is this a subversive challenge to Elizabeth's political philosophy, to the underpinnings of the Tudor state in the 1590s? To these considerations one might add the topicality many scholars have argued by drawing parallels between John and Elizabeth, Arthur and Mary Queen of Scots, Hubert and Secretary Davison, whom Elizabeth had asked to murder Mary. The similarities indicate a provocative, even a dangerous, interrogation of the very recent past.[6] On the other hand, one may regard John's anachronistic bravado as a playful exploitation of the contemporaneity of all history. For a moment in the play, John stretches his rhetorical muscle and becomes the true English monarch, appropriating Tudor mythology in the service of patriotism. The playwright can depend upon the anti-Catholicism and Armada nationalism of some large part of his audience for the anticipated response; moreover, at least for this theatrical moment, John's rhetoric places the Tudor parallel in a favorable light which cuts across the subversive connections which justify the political expediency of eliminating one's enemies by any means available. Perhaps even more immediate might be the impression that the usurping king is once again improvising a display of sovereignty, language his only instrument of power apart from military force.

Any number of other scenes ironically displace contemporary aspects of ideology, orthodoxy, and presentational politics in locations which reveal paradoxical disjunctions of language and action: Petrarchan politics in the decadent French court, Christian humanism from the ineffective Henry VI, providentialism from the hysterical Queen Margaret, chivalric loyalty from the bloodthirsty Clifford, the divinity of kings from Richard III, dynastic diplomacy from Lewis of France. The privileged script royalty's theory and prerogatives require it to act out is altered radically when a Jack Cade mounts the stage of politics; the insecure John's boasting manifests the absence of any script and the mad "tug and scamble" to improvise power from the scraps of majesty and pomp. Neither abrogates nor discredits the understandable rage for order at the center of the iconic, institutional, and ideological assumption of political stability, yet both dramatize the chaos of uncertainties awaiting its efforts to embody the timeless within the timebound moment of the confusion and chaos of history.

These paradoxes of rule and of the public theater's representation of history remain vital parameters for the Second Tetralogy's explorations of statesmanship and anarchy. Nastiness and savagery still characterize the political world, and military force and unprincipled expediency guide men's actions. Like York, Richard III, and John, Richard II and Bolingbroke adopt the use of a loyal supporter to kill off an opponent and then deny complicity with the intermediary. Although the shifting loyalties of the later plays are harder to follow without the red and white roses to cue us, they do vary previous patterns of alienating the powerful nobles and dramatize the forming and reforming of alliances. Many of the basic premises are shared by both tetralogies, but the second more rapidly sketches in the nightmarish jungle of political expediency at the beginning of *Richard II* and moves on to other interests. With the exception of Richard's confiscation of Gaunt's estates, his abuses of royal prerogative – including the elimination of Woodstock – occur before the opening of the play: discriminating between the exercise of power and the display of power becomes immediately problematic.

Acting the king becomes the central concern of the later history plays and requires a continuous and sophisticated self-consciousness.[7] Richard II fails partly because he understands politics as performance as merely the self-satisfied presentational display of a privileged script. His Lancastrian successors accept politics as paradox and work out their own versions of theatrical politics; both accept the fact that the king's role is a dramatic construction. Though beset by other paradoxes, especially those involving the past rebellion of the present king, Henry IV limits the presentational complexity of theatricalizing his appearances to majesty seen in its dazzling glory from a distance; he sees the necessity of manipulating the symbolic structures of kingship but is powerless to create its drama.

Prince Hal recognizes the paradoxes of theatrical politics as a burden but also embraces them as necessity and as opportunity. He recognizes the role of king as representation as well as presentation: a dramatic construction which does not become fixed as an icon for display but which must move because history moves and politics is essentially dramatic. The king's role does not cease to be iconographic, institutional, ceremonial, ideological, but those static elements of playing the part must find a stage and a script in which Hal's representation of the king can be presented imaginatively and dramatically. He discovers that questions of legitimation do not necessarily disappear when his dramatic construction of the king's role captures his subjects' imaginations, but they do become more manageable; he discovers that he must improvise within the paradoxes of politics, playing with the traditions and ceremonies, balancing them against the human and historical, presenting the king as timeless icon and representing the truth that life is timebound and therefore dramatic.

The politics at play in these paradoxes deepens the sense of the stage of history and complicates the response to the theatricality of the early history plays, the public theatre, and Elizabethan culture. That response involves the audience's self-consciousness as subjects of the English monarch, a role they play within and outside the public theater, one which implicitly requires its own dramatic choices, improvizations, and constructions within its own interpretation of the paradoxes of politics.

Notes

All quotations from the early history plays are from the Arden editions. Passages from other Shakespeare plays are quoted from *The Riverside Shakespeare*, ed. G. B. Evans.

CHAPTER 1: THEATRE, HISTORY, POLITICS

1. This point has often been made, particularly in response to the adaptation of the methods of New Criticism to the drama. See, for example, John Russell Brown's "Theatre Research and the Criticism of Shakespeare and His Contemporaries," *Shakespeare Quarterly*, 13 (1962), reprinted in his *Shakespeare's Plays in Performance* (Baltimore: Penguin, 1969 [1966]), 237–52.
2. A number of interesting discussions of the role of the Shakespearean director would take us further into the question but away from our plays. But see Richard David's brief comments on the director as cook in his *Shakespeare in the Theatre* (Cambridge: Cambridge University Press, 1978), 13–16, and John Russell Brown's *Free Shakespeare* (London: Metheun, 1974).
3. So David Daniell remarks, near the conclusion of a long review: "Having watched these three plays several times, I am not aware of the 'Tudor myth' at all, nor of any Providential process . . . . " See "Opening up the text: Shakespeare's *Henry VI* plays in performance," in *Drama and Society*, ed. James Redmond. Themes in Drama, I (Cambridge: Cambridge University Press, 1979), 274.
4. Brown calls attention to this scene's importance and remarks: "The unanimity of the reviewers in paying tribute to the playing of this scene in the 1951 production [at Stratford] should be recorded in order to direct the literary critic's attention towards a significant feature of the play's theatrical life, a scene which gives a still centre in personal affection, to the round of wars, distrust and self-aggrandisement." *Shakespeare's Plays in Performance*, 249.
5. Warren, "Comedies and Histories at Stratford, 1977," *Shakespeare Survey*, 31 (1978), 150; Daniell, "Opening up the text," 274.
6. *The Shakespeare Revolution* (Cambridge: Cambridge University Press, 1977), 8.
7. Roberts, "Shakespeare in Washington, D. C.," *Shakespeare Quarterly*, 30 (1979), 196; Dennis Bartolomeusz, "Shakespeare in Sydney and Melbourne," *ibid.*, 267.
8. "Plays in Performance," *Drama*, no. 103 (1971), 31.
9. "On Producing *Henry VI*," *Shakespeare Survey*, 6 (1953), 50.

10. "Shakespeare, the Twentieth Century, and 'Behaviorism,'" *Shakespeare Survey*, 20 (1967), 139.

11. Irving Wardle's review in *The Times*, 13 July 1977, quoted in Ralph Berry, *Changing Styles in Shakespeare* (London: George Allen and Unwin, 1981), 80–1. Berry's discussion of recent productions of *Henry V* provides a good example of the value of production-centered criticism – and of its limitations.

12. *Shakespeare's Plays Today* (London: Sidgwick and Jackson, 1970), 43.

13. *Shakespeare in the Theatre*, 102.

14. "On Producing *Henry VI*," 49.

15. "*King Henry VI, Part 2*: Notes During Production," *Theatre Annual*, 13 (1955), 45–6.

16. Stephen Greenblatt has labelled this new direction in the study of the English Literary Renaissance "the new historicism." See his "Introduction" to *The Power of Forms in the English Renaissance* (Norman, Oklahoma: Pilgrim Books, 1982), 3–6, for a discussion of its challenges to traditional literary interpretation. Greenblatt's *Renaissance Self-Fashioning: From More to Shakespeare* (Chicago: University of Chicago Press, 1980) is a central text in an increasingly influential approach to reading the politics of Elizabethan writers.

    Two recent collections of essays offer helpful examples of how to assess the ideology of literary texts: *Alternative Shakespeares*, ed. John Drakakis (London: Methuen, 1985) and *Political Shakespeare: Essays in Cultural Materialism*, ed. Jonathan Dollimore and Alan Sinfield (Manchester: Manchester University Press, 1985). See also Sinfield's "Power and Ideology: An Outline Theory and Sidney's *Arcadia*," *ELH*, 52 (1985), 259–77, for a provocative approach to uniting theory and interpretation. Edward Pechter has attempted to assess its importance and to evaluate its assumptions and presumptions in "The New Historicism and Its Discontents: Politicizing Renaissance Drama," *PMLA*, 102 (May 1987), 292–303.

17. Shakespeare's contemporaries were clearly aware of the subversive qualities of the stage. See M. C. Bradbrook, *The Rise of the Common Player* (Cambridge, Mass.: Harvard University Press, 1964); Jonas Barish, *The Anti-Theatrical Prejudice* (Berkeley: University of California Press, 1981); and especially Louis Adrian Montrose, "The Purpose of Playing: Reflections on a Shakespearean Anthropology," *Helios*, 7 (1980), 51–74. See the following section of this chapter for a more thorough discussion.

18. See, for example, Lily B. Campbell, *Shakespeare's Histories: Mirrors of Elizabethan Policy* (London: Methuen, 1964 [San Marino: The Huntington Library, 1947] and F. O. Levy, *Tudor Historical Thought* (San Marino: The Huntington Library, 1967).

19. E. M. W. Tillyard, *The Elizabethan World Picture* (London: Chatto and Windus, 1943) and *Shakespeare's History Plays* (New York: Collier Books, 1962 [London: Chatto and Windus, 1944]).

20. See Jonathan Dollimore and Alan Sinfield, "History and Ideology: The Instance of *Henry V*," in *Alternative Shakespeares*, 206–9. My view differs from but is not really opposed to Dollimore and Sinfield's.

21.   For example, Andrew S, Cairncross, ed., *King Henry VI, Part I*, Arden edition (London: Methuen, 1962), xli; Alvin Kernan in *The Revels History of Drama in English. Volume III: 1576–1613* (London: Methuen, 1975), 264; Gareth Lloyd Evans, *The Upstart Crow: An Introduction of Shakespeare's Plays* (London: J. W. Dent, 1982), 1–3.

22.   "The literature of the Elizabethan Age, as a matter of course, reflected this class structure as frequently and as innocently as our literature reflects that of the twentieth century," writes David L. Stevenson, "Introduction" to *The Elizabethan Age*, ed. Stevenson (Greenwich, Conn.: Fawcett, 1966), 16.

23.   The paradox that ideology reveals its vulnerability as it displays itself has attracted the attention of recent critics and theorists; see, for example, Dollimore and Sinfield, "History and Ideology: The Instance of *Henry V*"; Greenblatt, "Invisible Bullets: Renaissance Authority and Its Subversion, *Henry IV* and *Henry V*," in *Political Shakespeare*, 18–47; and the general essay by Pierre Macherey and Etienne Balibar, "On Literature as an Ideological Form: Some Marxist Propositions," *Oxford Literary Review*, 3 (1978), 4–12.

24.   See, for example, the recent collection of re-evaluations, *The Reign of Elizabeth I*, ed. Christopher Haigh (Athens: University of Georgia Press, 1985).

25.   Keith Wrightson has strongly presented the case for decentering the history of the period; he concludes that "The impact of social change in late sixteenth- and seventeenth-century England presents itself to the historian as a series of localized social dramas." *English Society: 1580–1680* (London: Hutchinson, 1982), 222.

26.   Tillyard, *Shakespeare's History Plays*, 39–40.

27.   For a concise statement of Henry VII's strategy, see the discussion by Lacey Baldwin Smith in his *This Realm of England: 1399–1688*, Fourth Edition (Lexington, Mass.: D. C. Heath, 1983), 93–7.

28.   In a series of studies, Anthony Giddens has presented a very provocative theory of social action. His examination of this pattern of dominance/ resources/ transformative capacity applies this model of power as relational to social theory in general and in no way links it with the Elizabethan or even the early modern period. See Giddens' *Central Problems in Social Theory* (Berkeley: University of California Press, 1979). I here acknowledge my indebtedness to this and other works by Giddens, whose theories I have freely adapted.

29.   This is the assumption that dominates much of Greenblatt's analysis in *Renaissance Self-Fashioning* and "Invisible Bullets." It also is prevalent elsewhere in *Political Shakespeare* and *The Reign of Elizabeth I*. For a criticism of Greenblatt, see Alan Sinfield, "Power and Ideology" (note 1 above), 259–65.

30.   The treatise was *The Discoverie of a gaping gulf whereinto England is like to be swallowed by another French mariage, if the Lord forbid not the banes by letting her majestie see the sin and punishment thereof.* Sinfield comments on the Stubbs case, and a fuller analysis of *The Gaping Gulf* is in Wallace T. MacCaffrey's *Queen Elizabeth and the Making of Policy, 1572–1588* (Princeton: Princeton University Press,

1981), 255–62.

31. Camden's work is most conveniently sampled in the selections edited by Wallace MacCaffrey, *The History of Princess Elizabeth, Late Queen of England* (Chicago: University of Chicago Press, 1970). The quotation is from 138–9.

32. Camden, *Princess Elizabeth*, 139; MacCaffrey, *Quenn Elizabeth and the Making of Policy*, 257. The lawyer, Dalton, was freed from the Tower in 1581; the printer, Singleton, was pardoned at the time.

33. Sidney, *Miscellaneous Prose*, ed. Katherine Duncan-Jones and Jan van Dorsten (Oxford: Clarendon Press, 1973), 33. For comment upon Stubbs and Sidney, see Sinfield, "Power and Ideology," 259-60, 274–5.

34. Keith Wrightson offers this summary: "Pressure from above for the creation of a more ordered and stable society could never have more than a very limited and temporary success if it was not accompanied by, and in broad conformity with, spontaneous local efforts to meet the needs and respond to the problems of the age. Government directives, as we have seen, had to pass through a filter of local interests before finding implementation in the counties. Similarly, at a more intimately local level, the attempts of the magistracy to put into execution the desires of the royal government could founder where they were not complemented by a ground swell of local support." *English Society: 1580–1680*, 155.

35. For a re-assessment of Elizabeth's attitudes and policies, see Patrick Collinson, "The Elizabethan Church and the New Religion," in *The Reign of Elizabeth I*, ed. Haigh, 169–94.

36. On Leicester as a politician, see especially MacCaffrey, *Queen Elizabeth and the Making of Policy*, 440–8, and Simon Adams, "Eliza Enthroned? The Court and Politics," in *The Reign of Elizabeth I*, ed. Haigh, 55–78. Sir John Neale describes a factional relationship between Leicester and Cecil in his British Academy Raleigh Lecture of 1948, reprinted in *Essays in Elizabethan History* (London: Jonathan Cape, 1958), 84 ff. The degree of their opposition as well as the problems of defining "faction" during this period are reassessed by Simon Adams, "Faction, Clientage, and Party: English Politics, 1550–1603," *History Today*, 32 (December 1982), 33–9. Adams' definition of "faction" as essentially one of "personal rivalry" (34) does not seem to square with Sir Philip Sidney's warning about factionalism in his letter to Elizabeth of 1579; in *Miscellaneous Prose*, 47.

37. This incident remains somewhat obscure, alluded to briefly by M. C. Bradbrook in *The Rise of the Common Player* (Cambridge, Mass.: Harvard University Press, 1964), 255 and 313 n. 6. See also D. Cressy, "Binding the Nation: the Bonds of Association, 1584 and 1696," in *Tudor Rule and Revolution*, ed. D. J. Ruth and J. W. McKenna (Cambridge: Cambridge University Press, 1982), 217–26. Christopher Haigh writes that "Its conception and organization show an astonishing lack of confidence in the mechanisms of government and in the breadth of support which the regime enjoyed" and concludes that "The realities of the Elizabethan polity had been laid bare." In

his "Introduction" to *The Reign of Elizabeth I*, 17.

38. "All the conventions of a highly formalized court asserted the unique and lofty authority of the monarch and the submissive role of the subject. Yet these conventions barely served to veil the unceasing and often bitter struggle between royal and conciliar wills," writes Wallace T. MacCaffrey. "Place and Patronage in Elizabethan Politics," in *Elizabethan Government and Society*, ed. S. T. Bindoff, Joel Hurstfield, and C. H. Williams (London: Athlone Press, 1961), 97.

39. "The reasons for the queen's relative success are many and complex; they may be summarized by observing that it did not seem in the interest of a substantial segment of the population to attempt to demystify the queen's power, and hence it was enormously difficult to do so." Stephen Greenblatt, *Renaissance Self-Fashioning*, 166.

40. For the images of Elizabeth, see Frances A. Yates, *Astraea: The Imperial Theme in the Sixteenth Century* (London: Routledge and Kegan Paul, 1975) and Roy C. Strong, *The Cult of Elizabeth* (London: Thames and Hudson, 1977).

41. Quoted in J. E. Neale, *Elizabeth I and Her Parliaments, 1584–1601* (London: Jonathan Cape, 1965), II, 119.

42. In his *History of Richard III*, ed. R. S. Sylvester, *The Complete Works of Sir Thomas More* (New Haven: Yale University Press, 1980), III, 80.

43. The most thorough treatment of Elizabethan efforts to regulate the theater is Glynne Wickham's in his *Early English Stages, 1300 to 1660*. 2 vols in 3 parts (London: Routledge and Kegan Paul, 1959–72), II, pt. 2, 54–149. Notes below will refer to these volumes as Wickham, *EES*.

44. The interrelationship of patronage and letters in Elizabethan and Jacobean England has been shown to be much more complex than previously thought, as scholars have demonstrated that even the language of poetry was influenced by court politics and personalities and by an intricate configuration of elements which more often suggest a maze than a system. In any case, the intentions varied with the sponsoring Court or regional aristocrat, and seldom is artistic patronage free from the larger maze of political patronage. For recent perspectives, see the essays in *Patronage in the Renaissance*, ed. Guy Fitch Lytle and Stephen Orgel (Princeton: Princeton University Press, 1981), especially Arthur F. Marotti's "John Donne and the Rewards of Patronage" and Leonard Tennenhouse's "Sir Walter Ralegh and the Literature of Clientage."

45. Gosson, *Plays Confuted in Five Actions*. Facsimile edition (New York: Johnson Reprint, 1972), sigs. C5, G6–G7.

46. For the post-Reformation attitudes toward images and its influence on Elizabethan poetics, see Greenblatt, *Renaissance Self-Fashioning*, esp. 188–91; John Siemon, *Shakespeare's Iconoclasm* (Berkeley: University of California Press, 1985); Michael O'Connell, "The Idolatrous Eye: Iconoclasm, Antitheatricalism, and the Image of the Elizabethan Theater," *ELH*, 52 (1985), 279–310.

47. For the apparel given by noblemen to their servants, who in turn

sold it to the players (where could servants wear such finery?), see *Thomas Platter's Travels in England, 1599,* trans. Clare Williams (London: Jonathan Cape, 1937), 167. For incidents of the sale of clerical vestments, see Wickham, *EES,* II, part 1, 38–9.

48. See David Bevington's helpful comments about the interrelationships of costume, spectators' interpretive expectations, the morality plays' didacticism, and the later drama's "putting theatrical entertainment and illusion ahead of certainty of meaning"; in *Action Is Eloquence: Shakespeare's Language of Gesture* (Chicago: University of Chicago Press, 1984), 35–40.

49. On the survival and transformation of such villains as the Vice and Sedycyon in Shakespeare's plays, see Robert Weimann, *Shakespeare and the Popular Tradition in the Theater,* ed. Robert Schwartz (Baltimore: The Johns Hopkins University Press, 1978), esp. 120–60.

50. On this development of self-consciousness and its potential subversiveness, see Louis Adrian Montrose, "The Purpose of Playing," esp. 57, 62–6.

51. The phrase is Roy C. Strong's in *Splendor at Court* (London: Thames and Hudson, 1975), Chapter 1.

52. *The Letters and Epigrams of Sir John Harington,* ed. Norman E. McClure (Philadelphia: University of Pennsylvania Press, 1930), 122. In *Renaissance Self-Fashioning,* Stephen Greenblatt also discusses this passage but draws different conclusions.

53. On this paradox, particularly enlightening is the essay by Pierre Macherey and Etienne Balibar, "On Literature as an Ideological Form."

54. On the audience's commanding "celebrations of royal power and assertions of aristocratic community," see Stephen Orgel's *The Illusion of Power: Political Theater in the English Renaissance* (Berkeley: University of California Press, 1975), Chapter 1, 1–36, esp. 5–7.

55. See Alvin B. Kernan, "Shakespeare's Stage Audiences: The Playwright's Reflections and Control of Audience Response," in *Shakespeare's Craft: Eight Lectures,* ed. Philip H. Highfill (Carbondale, Illinois: Southern Illinois University Press, 1982), 113–37. Kernan examines five plays within plays for what they tell us about Shakespeare's "theatrical epistemology."

56. Wickham, *EES,* II, part 1, 89–90.

57. My discussion in these paragraphs is indebted to Bernard Beckerman's "Historic and Iconic Time in Late Tudor Drama," in *Shakespeare, Man of the Theater,* eds. Kenneth Muir, Jay L. Halio, and D. J. Palmer. Proceedings of the Second Congress of the International Shakespeare Association, 1981 (Newark: University of Delaware Press, 1983), 37–44.

58. Greenblatt argues that "one of the highest achievements of power is to impose fictions upon the world and one its supreme pleasures is to enforce the acceptance of fictions that are known to be fictions." *Renaissance Self-Fashioning,* 141. Though this states the theatricality of rhetorical politics boldly, its dark cynicism obliterates the difference between Machiavellian violence and dynastic aesthetics.

59. Alessandro Serpieri provides a concise and provocative semiotic reading of the ideological conflicts involved in demythologizing of the "motivated Name" of Caesar and of the politicsof absolute sovereignty in *Julius Caesar* in "Reading the Signs:Towards a Semiotics of Shakespearean Drama," *Alternative Shakespeares*, ed. Drakakis, 119–43, esp. 125–34.

CHAPTER 2: HENRY VI, PART ONE

1. Andrew S. Cairncross's comments upon ceremony in the play are brief but suggestive; in his Arden introduction, lii-liii. On the general topic of ceremony I have found David Bevington's "The Language of Ceremony" helpful; *Action Is Eloquence*, ch. 5.
2. C. L. Barber, *Shakespeare's Festive Comedy* (Princeton: Princeton University Press, 1959), 193.
3. Cairncross links the opening scene with "the disasters of Job," xlvi; see also his note to the stage direction at the beginning of the play.
4. *1 Henry VI* has an earnestness which distinguishes it from most of the rather turgid and meaningless entertainments offeredon the public stages at the time of the Armada," writes M. M. Reese in *The Cease of Majesty: A Study of Shakespeare's History Plays* (London: Edward Arnold, 1961), 179.
5. *Narrative and Dramatic Sources of Shakespeare*, ed. Geoffrey Bullough (London: Routledge and Kegan Paul, 1957–75), III, 24–5. The topicality of *1 Henry VI* has received little attention, though A. L. Rowse has made the claim that "it was the war in Normandy – always closest to English hearts – that called forth *Henry VI*, gave it its success and started the career of the most popular dramatist of the time." The remark is made in passing in *The Expansion of Elizabethan England* (London: Macmillan, 1955), 397.
6. The figures for conscription are assembled in Appendix I of C. G. Cruickshank's *Elizabeth's Army*, 2nd ed. (Oxford: The Clarendon Press, 1966).
7. For Essex, see the *Dictionary of National Biography*, s.v. Robert Devereux, 2nd Earl of Essex, V. 873 ff. for the basic facts. Anthony Esler quotes a contemporary Frenchman's amusement at the English courtier-soldiers at the siege of Rouen: "armed and costumed like the antique figures shown on old tapestries, with coats of mail and iron helmets." From the Duc d'Angouleme's *Memoires*, 1 October 1589, in *The Aspiring Mind of the Elizabethan Younger Generation* (Durham: Duke University Press, 1966), 93. The absurdity of Essex's chivalry can be sampled in Walter Bourchier Devereux's *Lives and Letters of the Devereux, Earls of Essex*, 2 vols (London, 1853); see I, 273, for the challenge to a singlecombat. Bullough includes excerpts from Sir Thomas Coningsby's *Journal of the Siege of Rouen, 1591* in *Narrative and Dramatic Sources*, III, 80–6; Coningsby's sense of the spectacle, sport, and honor of war suggests the romanticizing of such campaigns by the aristocratic mind.

8. Alfred Harbage's statement may serve as an example of the older view of the play's simplicity: "[It] is a play about the courage, prowess, and assumed righteousness of the English as represented by such loyal and able leaders as Salisbury, Warwick, and, above all, Talbot; and about the opportunism, treachery, and fox-like successes of the French as represented by the fraud and moral depravity of La Pucelle." *As They Like It: A Study of Shakespeare's Moral Artistry* (New York: Harper Torchbooks,1961[1947]), 153. Cairncross says that "The theme of the play is the loss of France and the ruin of England." Arden Introduction, xlix.

9. See the later chapters. I have treated the comic grotesque less fully in "The Dark Comedy of the Henry VI Plays," *Thalia: Studies in Literary Humor*, 5 (1980), 11–21.

10. Ernest W. Talbert writes that "The comic process of 1 *Henry VI* is centered about Joan, and overtones of the comic occur when she first appears. The love rhetoric of Charles is amusing in its absurdity. It also agrees with a comic conception that will place Charles and Joan in situations reminiscent of the braggart and the prostitute, as well as the ugly, rustic, brawling wench." *Elizabethan Drama and Shakespeare's Early Plays* (Chapel Hill: University of North Carolina Press, 1963), 183. Talbert is one of the few critics who writes well of the comic in 1 *Henry VI*.

11. Wilson, *The Arte of Rhetoricke* (London, 1553), 135–6.

12. Bright, *A Treatise of Melancholie* (London, 1586), 82–3.

13. The English has embarked, Gareth Lloyd Evans writes, upon "a sea of national decadence," so that the French derision is justified. *Shakespeare I: 1564–1592* (Edinburgh: Oliver and Boyd, 1975), 37–9. Even the "barbs" of "Joan's searching indictment of English hypocrisy," as J. B. Brockbank points out, cannot "be removed by the spectacle of her converse with evil spirits." "The Frame of Disorder: *Henry VI*," in *Early Shakespeare*, ed. J. R. Brown and Bernard Harris, Stratford-upon-Avon Studies, 3 (London: Edward Arnold, 1961), 80.

14. Typical of the first view is, of course, Tillyard, but more recently see Alvin Kernan, who writes about the early histories as "rituals of the conservative view of history and the ethic of order, counselling obedience and submission to the old ways and showing the dreadful consequences of rebellion and usurpation." *The Revels History of Drama in English. Volume III: 1576–1613* (London: Methuen, 1975), 264. Still more recently Robert Rentoul Reed, Jr. argues that inherited guilt and divine retribution hold the two tetralogies together. *Crime and God's Judgment in Shakespeare* (Lexington: University Press of Kentucky, 1984).

Lawrence V. Ryan's introduction to the Signet edition of 1 *Henry VI* (New York: New American Library, 1967) provides an example of a Shakespeare who "brooded about the possibility that the cycle might recur, especially if men should ignore the lessons taught by history" (xxvi).

15. John W. Blanpied's examination of the elements of parody complements my sense of the comic in the play; see his "'Art and

Baleful Sorcery': The Counterconsciousness of 1 *Henry VI*," *Studies in English Literature*, 15 (1975), 213–27. Donald R. Wineke's view that Shakespeare is exploring a "Machiavellian landscape" is somewhat similar to mine; see "The Relevance of Machiavelli to Shakespeare: A Discussion of 1 *Henry VI*," *Clio*, 13 (1983), 17–36.

16. For a wide variety of examples of Shakespeare's significant use of images of kneeling, see David Bevington, *Action Is Eloquence*, 164–72.

17. Daniell, "Opening Up the Text: Shakespeare's *Henry VI* Plays "in performance," in *Drama and Society*, ed James Redmond. Themes in Drama, I (Cambridge: Cambridge University Press, 1974).

18. On the imagery of sexual inversion in the play, see David Bevington"s "The Domineering Female in 1 *Henry VI*," *Shakespeare Studies*, 2 (1967), 46–66.

19. Sidney, *Prose Works*, ed. Albert Feuillerat (Cambridge: Cambridge University Press, 1917–1924), III, 40.

20. Nashe, *Pierce Pennilesse, His Supplication to the Divell* (London, 1592), 87.

CHAPTER 3: HENRY VI, PART TWO

1. Almost invariably modern commentators have seen "the good Duke Humphrey" as a loyal and wise humanist, and no doubt he does support his king and does try several times to provide him with sound, judicious advice. We are sympathetic to Gloucester partly, I believe, because we see the others temporarily set aside their quarrels to conspire against him and eliminate his opposition to their several plans by deposing him from the protectorate, because Gloucester alone tries to help Henry, and because the play shows that the commoners admire him.

   After his murder, halfway through the play, the field is cleared for the unprincipled jockeying for power, but the Duke had actually done little to prevent violence and scheming in the first two acts. Perhaps Gloucester's "goodness" owes more to his own self-conception, the critic's need to find balanced structure, and the chronicle sources than to Shakespeare's portrait. Henry's uncle does see himself in the chroniclers' role as the invaluable Lord Protector, but Shakespeare undermines that self-conception by highlighting his choleric nature in the lengthy and divisive criticism of the marriage contract and in the various series of insults he trades with the other noblemen and especially with the Cardinal, both openly and behind the King's back. Michael Manheim has a point in asserting that "to the theater audience of the 1590s the image of the humanist is that of a loser in politics," but Gloucester's resistance to the "new Machiavels" is more passive than active (see Manheim's *The Weak King Dilemma in the Shakespeare History Play* [Syracuse: Syracuse University Press, 1973], 90–2.) Shakespeare's play challenges the humanist optimism about human nature and politics on a much broader scale, though certainly Gloucester's expectation of the triumph of justice marks him as naive and dooms him.

2. For a provocative discussion of the problematic relationships among representations of rebellious peasants, generic conventions, and history, see Stephen Greenblatt's "Murdering Peasants: Status, Genre, and the Representation of Rebellion," *Representations*, 1 (1983), 1–29.

3. The "liming" image also appears in the dying Cardinal's vision of Gloucester, the man he has murdered:

> He hath no eyes, the dust hath blinded them.
> Comb down his hair; look! look! it stands upright,
> Like lime-twigs set to catch my winged soul.
> (III.3.14–16)

4. *2 Henry VI* frequently uses morality play abstractions; see, for example, I.3.176, III.1.174, and III.2.299–303, 314.

5. Complementary to my discussion is Barbara Hodgdon's brief analysis of the shifting focus of Shakespeare's scenes in the play: from public to private and from groups to individuals. The alternations "increase audience awareness of the discrepancies between public, cosmetic 'shows' of love and duty and private, truthful, thoughts, feelings, and reactions." "Shakespeare's Directorial Eye: A Look at the Early History Plays," in *Shakespeare's More Than Words Can Witness: Essays on Visual and Nonverbal Enactment in the Plays*, ed. Sidney Homan (Lewisburg: Bucknell University Press, 1980), 120.

6. The discrepancies between action and rhetoric have become so broad that we need a better word than "ironic" to define the play's mode. "Nightmarish" suggests approaching the problems of the play as failures to control and to master anxiety; "pathogenic" might suggest approaching the origins of the lethal diseases of this society, the sources of the anxiety, yet these are less complex in the Henry VI plays.

7. Terry Hands' production emphasized the pathos and "mutual comfort" of King and Queen. David Daniell's review comments briefly upon the effectiveness of Hands' interpretation in "Opening Up the Text," 272–3.

8. Daniell describes this as the "first of two moving moments," the other coming at the end of IV.9; of this speech Daniell reports: "Alan Howard says it gently. Helen Mirren's reply startles him in her sudden strong truth of feeling as she quietly replies." *Ibid.*, 273.

9. David Riggs writes suggestively of York as "both the cause and the remedy of the condition he describes"; that is, York's ambition has created disruption within the commonwealth, but his strength and decisiveness offer the only cure for anarchy and validate his claim to the throne. See his discussion in *Shakespeare's Heroical Histories*, 125. J. P. Brockbank's assertion (in "The Frame of Disorder") also supports the approach taken here: "In *Henry VI* the sacrificial idea, which makes catastrophe a consequence of sin, is sharply

challenged by the 'machiavellian' idea that makes it a consequence of weakness."

10. Compare David Daniell, "Opening Up the Text," 265: "There are laughs, of course; but not many, and not the kind which the *Henry IV* plays get. There is unease in the audience; crisp playing only adds to the sense of simply *watching* matters get worse and worse so rapidly . . . . There is a little of the circus, too; but one of the achievements of this production is to get the sense of the largeness and closeness of the catastrophe, with much senseless slaughter all over the streets, and with half of London on fire. There develops, too, an alarming sense that the anarchy will begin to extend out into the audience."

11. On *Schadefreude*, see Erich Segal's "Marlowe's *Schadenfreude*: Barabbas as Comic Hero," in *Veins of Humor*, ed. Harry Levin, Harvard English Studies, 3 (Cambridge: Harvard University Press, 1972). For the tradition of combining the comic and terrible, see especially Muriel C. Bradbrook's discussion of the Marlovian grotesque in "Marlowe's *Doctor Faustus* and the Eldritch Tradition," *Essays on Shakespeare and the Elizabethan Drama*, ed. Richard Hosley (Columbia: University of Missouri Press, 1962), 83–90.

12. Eliot's phrase comes from "Notes on the Blank Verse of Christopher Marlowe," in *The Sacred Wood* (London: Methuen, 1920), 92.

13. Talbert writes that the "scene undoubtedly provided an amusing interlude for Elizabethans": "With comic irony Suffolk finds that the petition of a whole township is against himself for enclosing the commons, but he seizes upon Peter's petition as matter that can be used against York." *Elizabethan Drama and Shakespeare's Early Plays*, 194, 190.

14. Clifford Leech calls the scene "a grim comedy." "Moreover," he adds, "the formal combat between the armourer and his man is a parody of chivalric encounter: in a way remarkably sophisticated for this early drama, it implies a critical attitude towards the warring nobles whose quarrels are grotesquely mirrored in this fight between two simple men, one terrified, one drunk." *William Shakespeare: The Chronicles* (London: The British Council, 1962), 17.

15. Mock-battles and mock-combats were typical carnivalesque entertainments, ritualizations of aggression which were part of the institutionalization of disorder licensed by holiday. The practice during the Middle Ages and Renaissance is too widespread to require documenting, but Peter Burke's generalization will serve to express concisely the elements which this scene shares with the carnivalesque festivals: "The last act of the festival was often a drama in which 'Carnival' suffered a mock trial, made a mock confession and a mock testament, and was given a mock execution, usually by burning, and a mock funeral." *Popular Culture in Early Modern Europe* (New York: Harper Torchbooks, 1978), 185. No doubt, most of the Elizabethan audience had experienced such festivities and would have recognized Shakespeare's imitation of their form in the Horner-Peter combat.

16. *"King Henry VI: Part 2:* Notes During Production," *Theatre Annual,* 13 (1955), 45–6.

17. In "Murdering Peasants," Greenblatt argues that "Shakespeare depicts Cade's rebellion as a grotesque and sinister farce, the archetypal lower class revolt both in its motives and its ludicrousness" (23), but Cade's warped patriotism reveals at least the fragment of truth about the nobles' perfidy in losing France. Cade accuses Lord Say of the incompetence of the aristocracy's mismanagement of the great Henry V's conquest: "What canst thou answer to my Majesty for giving up of Normandy unto Monsieur Basimecu, the Dauphin of France? Be it known unto thee by these presence, even in the presence of Lord Mortimer, that I am the besom that must sweep the court clean of such filth as thou art" (IV.7.25–30).

18. For a general introduction to Carnival, Peter Burke's *Popular Culture in Early Modern Europe,* Chapter 7, provides basic information. I have summarized some of the essential features in "Erasmus' *Praise of Folly* and the Spirit of Carnival," *Renaissance Quarterly,* 32 (1979), 333–53. The primary synthesis of the various practices and the rationale behind them is Mikhail Bakhtin's *Rabelais and His World,* trans. Helene Iswolsky (Cambridge: M. I. T. Press, 1968). In the opening chapters of *Shakespeare's Festive Comedy* (Princeton: Princeton University Press, 1957), C. L. Barber gathers and analyzes much of the written evidence about folk festivals in Tudor England.

19. Greenblatt's interpretation should be noted here; he argues that "status relations . . . are being transformed before our eyes into property relations, and the concern . . . for maintaining social and even cosmic boundaries is reconceived as a concern for maintaining freehold boundaries. Symbolic estate gives way to real estate. And even in this revised context, the context of property rather than rank, the fear of stain in the representation of an unequal social encounter vanishes altogether." "Murdering Peasants," 25.

20. Arthur Freeman notes this discrepancy: "Shakespeare has also introduced the otherwise gratuitous episode of Iden's garden, a scene which may well bear cutting in a modern production. Iden himself remains an annoyingly loose end among disparate new faces in the last act: the man who announces himself loath to 'live turmoiled in the court' when he "may enjoy such quiet walks as these' in Kent . . . seems within a few lines overjoyed to attend henceforth upon King Henry at court: 'May Iden live to merit such a bounty!'" In his "Introduction" to the Signet edition of *Henry VI: Part Two* (New York: New American Library, 1967), xxxiii.

21. See Michael D. Bristol, "Carnival and the Institution of Theater in Elizabethan England," *English Literary History,* 50 (1983), 637–54.

CHAPTER 4: HENRY VI, PART THREE

1. My development of this understanding of the active energies of

chaos was suggested by some of M. M. Reese's comments upon the play; in *The Cease of Majesty*, 193 ff.

2. Daniell, "Opening up the text: Shakespeare's *Henry VI* plays in performance," in *Drama and Society*, ed. James Redmond. Themes in Drama, I (Cambridge: Cambridge Univeristy Press), 1979).

3. Jackson, "On Producing *Henry VI*," *Shakespeare Survey*, 6 (1953), 52.

4. See Daniell; also Roger Warren, "Comedies and Histories at Stratford, 1977," *Shakespeare Survey*, 31 (1978), 150. Ronald S. Berman's "Fathers and Sons in the Henry VI Plays" is helpful as well, *Shakespeare Quarterly*, 13 (1962), 487–97.

5. "The Frame of Disorder – *Henry VI*," in *Early Shakespeare*, 97–8.

6. Reese, *Cease of Majesty*, 206.

7. Jackson, "On Producing *Henry VI*," 49.

8. Brockbank, "The Frame of Disorder," 93.

9. "Three Kinds of Shakespeare," *Shakespeare Survey*, 18 (1965), 152.

10. Quoted by Homer D. Swander, "The Rediscovery of *Henry VI*," *Shakespeare Quarterly*, 29 (1978), 150.

11. Ibid.

12. *Shakespearean Iconoclasm* (Berkeley: University of California Press, 1985), 143.

13. I owe these connections to the suggestions of my colleague Peggy Goodman Endel, who is preparing a monograph on *Richard III* and the demonic imagery of Renaissance art and literature.

CHAPTER 5: RICHARD III

1. See Lamb's essay "Cooke's 'Richard the Third'" (1802) and his *On the Tragedies of Shakespeare* (1811); in *The Works of Charles Lamb*, ed. William McDonald (London: Dent, 1903), Vol. 3. The relevant excerpts are reprinted in the Signet Classic edition of *Richard III*, ed. Mark Eccles (New York: New American Library, 1964), 212–14.

2. *Angel with Horns and Other Shakespeare Lectures*, ed. Graham Storey (London: Longmans, 1961).

3. *Shakespeare and the Idea of the Play* (Harmondsworth: Penguin, 1967[1962]), 88.

4. Ironically, Richard functions as the only "moral" voice in the play, the "choric" characters wholly undermined by irony.
   On the roles that Richard plays, Wilbur Sanders's comments are suggestive: in *The Dramatist and the Received Idea* (Cambridge: Cambridge University Press, 1968), 89 ff. See also Michael Neill, "Shakespeare's Halle of Mirrors: Play, Politics, and Psychology in *Richard III*," *Shakespeare Studies*, 8 (1975), 99–129.

5. Neill, "Shakespeare's Halle of Mirrors," 111.

6. On Richard's manipulation of the symbols of royalty and their theatricality, see Bridget Gellert Lyons, "'Kings Games': Stage Imagery and Political Symbolism in 'Richard III'," *Criticism*, 20 (1978), 17–30.

7. *The Complete Works of St. Thomas More: Vol. 2: The History of Richard*

the Third, ed. Richard S. Sylvester (New Haven: Yale University Press, 1963), 80–1.

8. *King Richard III*, ed. Antony Hammond, Arden edition (London: Methuen, 1981), 105–6.

9. On the language of the play, Nicholas Brooke's analysis is very helpful: in his *Shakespeare's Early Tragedies* (London: Methuen, 1968), 48 ff.

10. Hammond, 110.

11. The prevailing critical attitude toward the play's politics is that it is crude melodrama; M. M. Reese, for example, comments that "*Richard III* is, from a purely political point of view, a less interesting play than *3 Henry VI*," a "popular" and a "splendid entertainment . . . because Shakespeare has relegated the political argument to the periphery of the action." *The Cease of Majesty*, 217, 225.

12. Understanding the place of factions at Elizabeth's court begins even before William Camden's *Annales*. Helpful are a number of recent essays by Simon Adams, "Faction, Clientage, and Party: English Politics, 1550–1603," *History Today*, 32 (December 1982), 33–9, and "Eliza Enthroned? The Court and its Politics," in *The Reign of Elizabeth I*, ed. Christopher Haigh (Athens: University of Georgia Press, 1985), 55–77; by Penry Williams, "Court and Polity under Elizabeth I," *Bulletin of the John Rylands University Library*, 65 (1973), 259–86; and by E. W. Ives, "Shakespeare and History: Divergencies and Agreements," *Shakespeare Survey*, 38 (1985), 19–35, esp. 21–5.

13. In presenting the factionalism of Edward IV's court and Richard's fears (even though they seem mock-fears for the most part), Shakespeare approximates the modern analysis of Richard of Gloucester's decision to take the throne; see the provocative summary in Jeffrey Richards, "The Riddle of Richard III," *History Today*, 33 (August 1983), 18–25.

14. *The Countess of Pembroke's Arcadia*, ed. Maurice Evans (Harmondsworth: Penguin, 1977), 766–7. See also Alan Sinfield, "Power and Ideology: An Outline Theory and Sidney's *Arcadia*," *English Literary History*, 52 (1985), 259–77.

15. The text of the 1597 edition is conveniently reprinted in the World Classics *Essays by Francis Bacon* (London: Oxford University Press, 1966[1937]), 243–69. See also F. J. Levy, "Francis Bacon and the Style of Politics," *English Literary Renaissance*, 16 (1986), 101–22.

16. Bacon, "Of Followers and Friends," *Essays*, 198.

17. Jonson, *Works*, eds. C. H. Herford and Percy Simpson (Oxford: Clarendon, 1922–52), I, 19, 139; cited by Jonathan Dollimore, "Transgression and Surveillance in *Measure for Measure*," in *Political Shakespeare*, eds. Dollimore and Sinfield, 81.

18. John Russell Brown, *Shakespeare's Plays in Performance*, 42.

19. Lines 65–8. The satires were composed in the 1590s, according to W. Milgate, whose edition I cite: *Satires, Epigrams, and Verse Letters* (Oxford: Oxford English Texts, 1967). On Donne at Court, Arthur F. Marotti provides an analysis which complements my discussion; see his "John Donne and the Rewards of Patronage," in *Patronage in*

the Renaissance, eds. Guy Fitch Lytle and Stephen Orgel (Princeton: Princeton University Press, 1981), 207–34.

20.   *Renaissance Self-Fashioning*, 140–1. For valuable appreciation and criticism of Greenblett's view, see Jonathan Goldberg, "The Politics of Renaissance Literature: A Review Essay," *English Literary History*, 49 (1982), 532 ff.

21.   Bridget Gellert Lyons offers a lengthier examination of this scene and concludes that "Visually, then, the scene is a highly effective one in which the throne, with its associations of legitimate authority, simply emphasizes by contrast Richard's crime and isolation, and his inability to sustain any kind of kingly language or gestures." "'Kings Games'," 25.

22.   Moody E. Prior, *The Drama of Power: Studies in Shakespeare's History Plays* (Evanston, Illinois: Northwestern University Press, 1973), 51.

23.   Brooke, *Shakespeare's Early Tragedies*, 78.

24.   The providential scheme – without the acknowledgment of *these* ironies – has appeared "repulsive" even to *Richard III*'s best critics; for example: Rossiter, *Angel with Horns*, 1–22; Brooke, *Shakespeare's Early Tragedies*, 78; Neill, "Shakespeare's Halle of Mirrors," 126.

CHAPTER 6: KING JOHN

1.   Freidrich Durrenmatt, *König Johan: Nach Shakespeare* (Zurich: Verlag der Arche, 1968), 33.

2.   The traditional chronology places the composition of *King John* in 1595–96, between the dates of *Richard III* and *Richard II*.
      The most convincing arguments for an earlier date are advanced by E. A. J. Honigmann in the New Arden edition of *King John* (London: Methuen, 1954), xliii–lviii. Honigmann believes that *John* was written "in the winter/spring of 1590/91." Wherever it falls in the chronology, *John* certainly belongs theatrically, structurally, and stylistically more with the plays of the first tetralogy than with the second. I personally favor the traditional chronology and the arguments of J. Dover Wilson in his New Cambridge edition, 1936, and of F. P. Wilson in his *Marlowe and the Early Shakespeare* (Oxford: University Press, 1953), 114–19.

3.   *Saturday Review*, 30 September 1899, 420; reprinted in the New Variorum *King John*, ed. H. H. Furness (Philadelphia and London: J. P. Lippincott, 1919), 687. The Variorum *John* also reprints a review by W. Winter of a 1909 production with Robert Mantell as King John. John was a "being prone to frightful wickedness, but not immune from equally frightful remorse." The opacity of John allows a certain latitude, though remorse is difficult to find in Shakespeare's text. Much more remorseful is the John of *The Troublesome Raigne*; see, for the best example, his dying speeches: Part 2, scene viii, lines 1040–90, in *Narrative and Dramatic Sources of Shakespeare*, ed. Geoffrey Bullough (London: Routledge and Kegan Paul, 1962), IV, 147–8. If *The Troublesome Raigne* is a source,

Shakespeare deliberately excised all John's remorse. Nevertheless, John's consciousness of the inevitable wretchedness of political realities seems to me warranted by Shakespeare's play.

4. See Adrian Bonjour, "The Road to Swinstead Abbey: A Study of the Sense and Structure of *King John*," *ELH*, 18 (1951), 261–3.

5. Honigmann says that John "tries to find everyone's price"; the Arden edition, lxviii. Some of the following remarks about John and Fortune are also indebted to Honigmann's introduction.

6. Pater, "Shakespeare's English Kings," in *Appreciations* (London: Macmillan, 1889), 189.

7. Jackson, "Shakespeare at Stratford, Ontario, 1974," *Shakespeare Quarterly*, 25 (1974), 399.

8. From Clarke's *Shakespeare's Characters* (London, 1863), quoted in the New Variorum, 678–9.

9. In the productions by the Royal Shakespeare Company in 1970 (directed by Buzz Goodbody) and in 1974 (directed by John Barton), John was played as manic, infantile, weak, and villainous.

10. In the New Variorum *John*, 328.

11. M. M. Reese, *The Cease of Majesty* (London: Edward Arnold, 1961), 280.

12. A. R. Humphreys, "The English History Plays," in *Shakespeare: Select Bibliographical Guides*, ed. Stanley Wells (London: Oxford University Press, 1973), 259.

13. Swinburne, *A Study of Shakespeare* (London: Heinemann, 1918 [1879]), 72.

14. See, for example, Bonjour's assertion that "John's career" is "tragic and admirable," that in the end he expiates himself, and that the final speeches of the Bastard and Prince Henry are "fittingly elevated and strangely moving, like a pardon giving last rest to a tormented soul." "The Road to Swinstead Abbey," 265.

15. See Eugene M. Waith, "*King John* and the Sense of History," *Shakespeare Quarterly*, 29 (1978), 194, n. 8.

16. See Alan Hughes, *Henry Irving, Shakespearean* (Cambridge: Cambridge University Press, 1981), 22. The other history plays among the frequently produced eleven were *Richard III*, *Henry V*, and *Henry VIII*.

17. The New Variorum *John*, 687–8.

18. Mark Van Doren comments that the bloated, declamatory "stuffiness of the prevailing style of *John*" is essential because the "theme of the play is excess." See his chapter on *John* in *Shakespeare* (Garden City: Anchor, 1953 [1939]), 88–97.

19. Reviewing Buzz Goodbody's RSC *John* of 1970, Peter Thomson objected to its playing for laughs: "Playing *King John* as if it were *Ubu Roi* led, not to a parody of the business of politics, but to a parody of the business of acting." "A Necessary Theatre: The Royal Shakespeare Season 1970 Reviewed," *Shakespeare Quarterly*, 24 (1971), 117–18.

20. Alan C. Dessen mentions this possibility of staging but only in passing during his discussion of "The Stage Psychomachia," in his

Elizabethan Drama and the Viewer's Eye (Chapel Hill: The University of North Carolina Press, 1977), 144–5.

21.   Reese, *The Cease of Majesty*, 279. Emrys Jones compares *John* with *Mundus et Infans* because both depict "the encounter between the inexperienced self and the world." *The Origins of Shakespeare* (Oxford: The Clarendon Press, 1977), 236.

22.   Ernest Schanzer comments briefly upon this aspect of the play's structure in *The Problem Plays of Shakespeare* (New York: Schoecken, 1963), 5–6.

23.   The substitution is discussed by Arthur Colby Sprague and J. C. Trewin in *Shakespeare's Plays Today* (Columbia: University of South Carolina Press, 1970), 27. Sprague and Trewin approve of the alteration, fearing the severed head might be laughed at.

24.   Shaw reports an interesting piece of Tree's stage business: "Little Arthur is plucking the daisies. The king smiles down at him as he passes, and the child starts away. There are some daisies growing near the spot where the king has been whispering his behest. Lightly he cuts the heads of them with his sword." The New Variorum *John*, 687. Even though this smiling nonchalance seems in keeping with the horror of John's request, and even though few would seriously attempt to whitewash John's criminality, such overt touches of sardonic evil threaten to make John into the consciously machiavellian Richard Crookback whom he only faintly resembles.

25.   *Shakespeare's Imagery and What It Tells Us*, 232.

26.   Introduction to the Arden edition, lxvii.

CHAPTER 7: PARADOX, PLAY, POLITICS

1.   A. P. Rossiter, *Angel with Horns* (London: Longmans, Green, 1951), especially "Ambivalence: The Dialectic of the Histories," 40–64, but also in his chapters on *Richard III* and *Richard II*. "Paradox" may seem a tired, traditional term, associated too closely with the New Critics' antipathy to extrinsic factors in interpretation; however, as Rossiter's analysis suggests, the sense of these plays as comic and ironic owes its origins to the nature of politics and history as well as to their treatment.

2.   Dollimore and Sinfield comment upon the paradox of ceremony in pointing to Henry V's torment over his "inability to ensure obedience": In IV.1. 240–57, Henry indicates a paradox of power only to misrecognize its force by mystifying both kingship and subjection. His problem is structural, since the same ceremonies or role-playing which constitute kingship are the means by which real antagonisms can masquerade as obedience – 'poison'd flattery.'" "History and ideology: the instance of *Henry V*," in *Alternate Shakespeares*, 218.

3.   Steven Mullaney's brief comments are helpful in analyzing the paradoxes of Elizabeth's theatrical politics; Mullaney emphasizes "the instability and especially the vulnerability inherent in a form of power that was, by necessity theatrically conceived, negotiated,

and maintained – a vulnerability to its own theatrically conceived conditions of possibility." "Brothers and Others, or the Art of Alienation," in *Cannibals, Witches, and Divorce: Estranging the Renaissance,* ed. Marjorie Garber, English Institute Essays, n.s. 11 (Baltimore: The Johns Hopkins University Press, 1987), 73. Again, the problem is structural.

4. James H. Kavanagh describes modern distinctions among kinds of discourse "unimaginable" for the Elizabethan and analyzes some of the ideological consequences of writing within such a unified social order. "Shakespeare in Ideology," in *Alternative Shakespeares*, 144–65, esp. 151 ff. Leonard Tennenhouse asks his readers "to imagine a situation where literary and political discourse had not yet been differentiated" and proceeds to describe many instances in which their identity reveals the ideological preoccupations of literature superficially innocent of political implication. *Power on Display: The Politics of Shakespeare's Genres* (London: Methuen, 1986), 2 *et passim.* If such critical awareness is crucial, equally important is the freedom this lack of clear demarcation allowed for *playing* with a language which seldom treated metaphor as belief or belief as metaphor because the two were not radically distinct.

5. On the openness of Elizabeth's court and its implication, see G. R. Elton, "Tudor Government; Points of Contact: the Court," in his *Studies in Tudor and Stuart Politics and Government* (Cambridge: Cambridge University Press, 1983), and David Loades, *The Tudor Court* (Totowa, New Jersey: Barnes and Noble, 1987).

6. See E. A. J. Honigmann's introduction to the Arden edition, xxvii–xxxiii, and Lily B. Campbell, *Shakespeare's Histories.*

7. John Barton stressed "acting the king" in his 1973 production at Stratford by casting Ian Richardson and Richard Pasco *both* as Richard II *and* Bolingbroke. Before I.1. began, the two would meet center-stage to decide who would play which role; though this addition emphasized another element of the comparison between the theater and the state as a stage and challenged traditional interpretations of Richard and Bolingbroke as opposites, Shakespeare's plays are never so metadramatically unsubtle. "Both actors," Helen Gardner comments," had to perform the difficult feat of acting persons who were only acting, and so not to be taken seriously." "Shakespeare in the Directors' Theatre," in her *In Defense of the Imagination,* (Cambridge, Mass.: Harvard University Press, 1982), 75.

Index